Rocks in My Head

Rocks in My Head

Celeste G. Engel

VANTAGE PRESS
New York / Atlanta
Los Angeles / Chicago

FIRST EDITION

All rights reserved, including the right of
reproduction in whole or in part in any form.

Copyright © 1987 by Celeste G. Engel

Published by Vantage Press, Inc.
516 West 34th Street, New York, New York 10001

Manufactured in the United States of America
ISBN: 0-533-07353-7

Library of Congress Catalog Card No.:86-91693

To my mother, Frances Gilpin,
and my grandmothers,
Marie Lauth and Ada Goodrich

Contents

Preface ix

I Had Him to Myself 1
A Salt Mine 5
Rattlesnakes 9
Bridge Games 12
Craps 16
Elengel 19
Field Trips 20
Talc Mines 28
Minerals 35
Natural Bridge 40
Pumpkins 44
Swamps 47
Death Valley 50
Caltech 55
Owl Creeks 62
Punch Bowl 69
On the Road Again 74
The Russians Are Coming 78
Chemistry 83
Grand Canyon 89
The Henry Mountains 94

Silica Accumulator Project	101
Scripps	107
Basalts	113
Crossings	120
Orly to Madagascar (Africa)	124
La Réunion	130
Mauritius	134
A Party	142
Dining at Sea	146
Twenty-four Hours	151
Depth Recording at Sea	157
Dredging	162
Trawling	167
Donovan	171
Pilots	175
Exit (Mozambique)	176
The Moon	180
Helen	187
Bill Otto	194
They Don't See the Rocks	200

Preface

My mother was a secretary at a fur company in Saint Louis, Missouri. She could spell well and she helped me a lot in spelling and in arithmetic. One day she came to our grade school with an umbrella for me. It was raining. I said, "Quick, how do you spell Constantinople?" She spelled it and I received an A.

My father was a bookkeeper. He and my mother had two daughters. I am the older and my father tried to fashion me into a son. He taught me to drive cars, trucks, and tractors. We fished and shot guns but we didn't kill anything except the fish we ate.

When I was in high school in Saint Louis, I knew I would go to college. It was expected and there was no negative discussion. Also, my grandmothers were determined that I be educated.

When I finished high school, they all sent me to the University of Missouri at Columbia. Grandmother told me that Mother cried for weeks because I was so far from home—about 150 miles.

"Perhaps she can get a husband there, if nothing else," they all said.

My father wanted me to go into the School of Business. I almost flunked out of school during the first course in accounting. We didn't have little calculators then, and through the long problems in addition and subtraction I could not balance debits and credits. My father gave up.

I liked science and told myself that I would go into the first science that I liked where I could be outdoors. I made better grades in zoology, but I ended up in geology, with a minor in history.

I was a graduate student in geology when the V-12 program of the U.S. Navy arrived on campus during World War II. I was supposed to teach those guys how to read a topographic map on the ground. We would get out into the field near a stream and hills, and then they would lie down and sleep or chew grass or just laugh at me, but I tried to teach them.

I was engaged to a star football player, but he planned to come back to Missouri and raise mules with his father. I love animals, all kinds, but not that much.

Then a geologist came to U.M. He worked for the U.S. Geological Survey on strategic minerals and came to the university to write a report on quartz crystals. Quartz (silicon dioxide), cut into thin wafers, was needed for radio sets. We were married in 1944, and I have worked with him most of my life.

Much later, almost in middle age, I went to UCLA for advanced degrees in geology. They would not take me until I had a lot more mathematics. I took the math courses. And I studied the Russian language so we could read what their geologists were doing. For me, Russian was more difficult than mathematics.

My husband and I have two grown sons. One is a biologist, the other an artist and attorney.

Rocks in My Head

I Had Him to Myself

Prof. Harold Urey came to the University of California, San Diego, about the same time my husband and I did in 1958. For a while he was at the Scripps Institution of Oceanography with us. Urey was internationally famous. He had isolated deuterium (heavy hydrogen), and for this he received the Nobel Prize in chemistry in 1934. Also, Urey developed methods for separating isotopes of uranium for our atomic bombs. He had many interests and had worked on numerous topics—for example, the origin of life, meteorites, the moon, and isotopes of oxygen, nitrogen, carbon, and sulfur. He had taught and trained a large group of students who were geochemists. At Scripps, Urey became interested in the chemistry of the rocks of the earth, but he was always looking skyward at the moon and other planets.

Urey was waiting for office and lab space in the new chemistry building on the upper campus at U.C. San Diego, but the place was not finished. He had a small office on the lower campus (Scripps), and on many days Urey ate lunch with us on the lawn, looking out to sea. He had to sit with the geologists at lunch.

We had a very mediocre lunch stand, so most everyone brought their lunches in bags. Urey was then a professor-at-large on the University of California campuses. As the title suggests, he could float around on any of the U.C. campuses, but he stayed in La Jolla most of the time. During lunchtime Urey would talk only about his work and what he was doing at the moment, so most of the men drifted away. However, I kept listening, because he fascinated me and I learned a lot. Finally, I did have him to myself.

When he was an undergraduate student, Urey studied forestry at the University of Montana in Missoula, Montana. One time I wrote to him from Montana and included a photo of a bolide, an exploding meteorite, that streaked across the western Montana sky. A man in the airport tower at Missoula snapped the photo. I heard the bolide, which sounded like exploding dynamite, but I did not look up into the sky. Actually, I thought it was dynamite set off by the Forest Service. The Forest Service was always up to no good.

Urey wrote back and thanked me for the photo and the Missoulian newspaper article. On the last line of his note he wrote: "What in the world are you doing there, in Montana?"

Before Urey went on to do graduate work, he earned some extra money teaching in a one-room school on the Musselshell River in central Montana. That must have been in 1918. In any event, he was in Montana so early that wolves followed him as he walked to school from his boardinghouse. When I looked alarmed, he said, "I just told them to go away, shoo, and they did."

His passion while I knew him well was for meteorites, particularly carbonaceous chondrites. He was fascinated by one specimen in particular, named Orgueil, which fell in France in the 1800s. Orgueil contained 3 to 5 percent free carbon, and of course, the excitement then was the possibility of finding fossil "life" in meteorites. He didn't tell me straight out, but Urey hoped to win another Nobel Prize. Very few people have won two Nobel Prizes. Linus Pauling won two prizes, one for chemistry and the second for peace.

A group of scientists came to work with Urey, and many others came to visit. They held a lot of seminars in which they speculated on the origin of life in the solar system. I went to everything. Some of the speakers had slides, thin sections of meteorites that they could project on a big screen, and we could see what they called organized elements, implying the origin of single-celled life. Some of this stuff turned out to be dust and pollen or other impurities that had fallen onto the musty shelves of the French museum where the Orgueil meteorite had been stored.

Then Urey gave me some prepared slides to look at under my petrographic microscope. This Orgueil meteorite was fragile. It had a glassy coating where the surficial minerals had melted as the meteorite came through the Earth's atmosphere. But you could crush the rest of it between your fingers. Lately, since the probes of various countries examined Halley's Comet, a few scientists are suggesting that carbonaceous chondrites came from the solid parts of comets.

I looked at and studied the minerals. They were all what geologists call secondary minerals, altered from normal, higher-temperature silicate minerals by water and gases.

Orgueil contained dolomite (Ca-Mg carbonate), gypsum (Ca-sulfate + water) and hydrated magnesium silicates, serpentine, talc, and chlorite, and a lot of junk minerals and that black stuff, organic or inorganic carbon.

I said, "Professor Urey, this is an altered rock from an asteroid in the solar system. It just can't be primary, pristine, first-order material from the beginning of the universe."

Urey was very annoyed with me. He said, "Celeste, you must stop thinking as if you are on the Earth." How could I?

I gave up, too.

Some scientists who study meteorites think that these carbonaceous chondrites are the primordial materials from which the planets formed. That seems backwards to me and inside out, so I don't think about it anymore.

Urey and his wife, Frieda, had a lovely home in La Jolla, where they had a lot of space to garden. Harold and Frieda entertained a lot.

I remember one dinner at their home very well, not for the food, but for the company. When we sat down there were four Nobel laureates and four of the rest of us. Maria Mayer, Linus Pauling, Harold Urey, and Chandrasekhar were the prizewinners. I sat next to Pauling and across from Maria. Maria had had a mild stroke, some time back, and Pauling studied her through dinner. Finally, Pauling reached into his jacket pocket and pulled out a tablet of niacin (100 mg.) and told Maria to take one tablet daily. Then he added, "Stop eating salt." I don't know what Maria did, but I started taking niacin immediately and dumped our box of salt into the trash.

This journey through the earth sciences was often dull, sometimes exciting, often frustrating, but on the whole fascinating.

A Salt Mine

Professor Branson, a specialist in invertebrate fossils—fossils of animals without backbones—was the first geologist I met who was kind to women students. Most professors in geology at the University of Missouri at that time were antiwomen. However, that may be too harsh a statement, because a lot of the younger faculty were gone, either in the military or involved in projects for the government in World War II.

Most of the female geologists were trained in micropaleontology, which is the study of tiny fossils that can be identified only under a microscope. The lucky students were able to get positions with oil companies in Texas.

In the spring of 1943, Branson asked me out for dinner at his home, and I knew I would have to help him weed the iris garden (magnificent) and drain the fish pool and clean it for the summer. We started in the iris garden, thinning the bulbs and pulling all the weeds. We couldn't finish on the first weekend, and I never made it back for the second weekend. The garden was alive with chiggers—millions of them, I would guess. In case you don't know about chiggers, they are tiny mites that burrow into the skin, particularly where the clothes are tighter, as in the waistband of underwear and along your brassiere, under arms and knees, and in socks around the ankle.

Of course, I knew about chiggers from living in Missouri, but I had forgotten them on that weekend. By Monday, I was a mass of itchy welts everywhere. The trick is not to scratch, but it takes these creatures at least a week to complete their life cycle in your body and then die. I haven't followed the literature on chiggers, but I do hope there is some cure now, short of immersing yourself in "flowers of sulfur."

After the work on the iris garden and fish pool, we went inside for a marvelous dinner prepared by Mrs. Branson. She was a very gracious lady.

During dinner, Professor Branson asked me if I wanted to attend geology camp in the Wind River Mountains of Wyoming. The university operated a field camp for our students and for geology students from other universities. We had students from all over the country. He told me that I could defray expenses by driving the bus or truck going to Wyoming and also by cooking breakfast every other day at the field camp.

"Yes, I want to go very much." I was full of enthusiasm. I knew I could drive any of the vehicles, but I couldn't cook at all.

My maternal grandmother, an angel, had lived with us while I was growing up. She was always cooking and saying to me, "Wait, I want to show you how to cook this. You will never get a husband if you can't cook."

The rest of the semester crawled by, and finally we were loaded to go from Columbia, Missouri, to Lander, Wyoming. We had an old bus and a truck that carried our extra clothes and sleeping blankets. Most students were too poor to have a sleeping bag, but two girls from Stanford and several from SMU had really fine boots, classy field clothes, and sleeping bags. All of us from Missouri had just two blankets rolled up together and tied with rope. We also had Dr. Branson in his old Buick and five extra students in that car.

It is strange that I can't remember much about the bus. It was not a school-bus size, but it was larger than a Carryall or the truck. Later, in the West, we had to push it a lot to get it started, so it was not very heavy. We had three male students and about twelve females from Missouri. The other students would join us in Wyoming.

I started out in the front seat of Professor Branson's Buick. The parking lot of the geology building was two levels below the street level. Branson always started out in high gear no matter where we were or how heavily loaded. The old Buick never failed. It climbed up the hill out of the parking lot in high gear with just a bit of sputtering. Remember, this trip started out in 1943, and there really wasn't much traffic on the highways. If Branson drove today in our present mess of traffic, we would have been dead.

First, as Branson drove along and found something to show us, instead of slowing or stopping, he took both hands off the wheel and waved his arms. I was terrified and tried to reach for the wheel across the student between us. Second, after lunch on warm days Branson would start to doze while driving. Everyone became nervous about that. Sometimes we wandered around across the line or onto the shoulder, but he usually awakened and guided us back onto the road. On the second day, I could see that the old Buick was used to driving Branson around, but I offered to drive for him, so that he could pay total attention to the terrain we were passing.

After we got him out from behind the wheel, the trip went a bit better. In western Kansas, we stopped to see fence posts sawed out of Niobrara chalk, I believe. (I am too lazy to look it up.) Of course, it was unique to see natural stone posts holding up barbed wire, but there were no trees to cut for posts, just miles and miles of sage brush and prairie grass and no traffic at all except an occasional truck.

We were in western Kansas headed due west on old

Highway 40, in the sagebrush, when Dr. Branson said, "Turn in here." A group of low metal buildings were grouped around piles and piles . . . of salt, as it turned out.

Dr. Branson said, "We will go into this salt mine."

Most everyone became very excited. Going into a mine certainly beat driving for days and days, and it did break the monotony. However, one girl crawled into the backseat of the bus and lay down on the seat. She didn't want to go into a mine, and Branson didn't miss her. A lot of people don't want to go into mines.

This was such an extraordinary mine that I can still taste the salt in the air. Every breath was another taste of salt. We went underground on a large square elevator in a vertical shaft, and we were not very deep. This must have been one of the last mines where the mine cars were pulled by mules. They were big, sleek, black animals, and that is why the elevator was so large. The mules worked six months underground, and then they were hoisted to the surface and given six months in the daylight.

The mine had electricity and was brilliantly lighted. All the crystal faces of salt reflected the light back at us. It could have been a mine full of diamonds instead of salt. At the working head of the drift, the miners were sawing the salt, first at the ceiling, which was a hard clay, and then near the floor of the bed. The bed of salt that they were mining was about seven feet thick. After sawing the top and bottom of the bed, they drilled small holes and broke the salt loose with dynamite. The salt was predominantly halite ($NaCl$), but there was some sylvite (KCl), which was pink. They tried to keep it separated from the white salt because KCl is bitter, but the salt was partially deformed. It had flowed into swirls, so that pink KCl was whipped into some white salt. The mine wall looked like a pale strawberry sundae.

I can't remember if it was road salt, table salt, or salt for the chemical industry, but that salt mine was the cleanest and driest mine I have ever seen, and I have seen more than my share of mines. We stuffed our pockets with chunks of salt. This area of Kansas had been covered millions of years ago by a large inland sea, which naturally was very salty. When the water dried up, it left this thick layer of commercial salt.

We all patted the mules good-bye. They had stalls filled with fresh straw and hay to eat, plus grain and vitamins to keep them healthy. Still it would be a terrible place to have to live for six months of days and nights.

Then we piled into the vehicles again and continued west toward Wyoming. The next day we saw the mighty Rocky Mountains. If you have lived all your life in Missouri, the first sight of the Rockies from the plains of eastern Colorado is a heavenly experience.

Rattlesnakes

Since I was a part-time cook at the geology camp in Wyoming and did not go out with the regular field geology course students, I was tutored every other day by Professor Branson. He and I took a lot of one-day field trips.

One morning, Branson decided to show me the fossils in the Cambrian formation (about 500 million years old) that was exposed halfway up a canyon. So we started out with our lunch in bags. I was worried about him because he had had several heart attacks. We were high, about seven thousand feet. He had some sort of map, but he claimed to know where we were going without it.

Well, this sort of trap would not be on a map anyway. We got into a crisscross fall of Lodgepole pine. It was simply dreadful, it was so dense. It wasn't high enough to crawl under and was too high to crawl over. We struggled for the next five hundred feet, first on big logs, then down in deep holes between logs. Today I think of all that waste firewood, but no one would bother to saw it up then. Branson didn't say much and neither did I. We had to rest a lot, usually in the holes beneath the logs.

I knew my legs soon would be covered with giant bruises, because I am not graceful and I kept falling over logs and crashing into other logs.

We ate our lunch in one of the holes, without water. Lunches were always peanut butter and honey sandwiches, which are as dry as dust in an arid country.

Branson gave up and we started back toward the car—the same trip, more falls and bruises. Near the car, on the other side of the road, was a cliff with a thin, shaley layer, and this sediment contained the brachiopods Branson was hunting (linguloids). So we did find the brachiopods after all, and they were very near the road.

Geologists, who should never get lost, do get lost—well, not lost exactly, just slightly bewildered, but they try to take short cuts, which end up in long marches on foot when the best exposure of rock is near the road. They often make a geologic field trip into a survival course.

Brachiopods have almost disappeared. They were bivalve creatures, with concave-convex shells without much meat in between. These were in the Gros Ventre formation. This one type, the linguloid, has survived as the Methuselah of all fossil brachiopods and lives today some 500 million years later in small areas of the oceans.

On another day, Branson drove me down the canyon and out onto the dry, parched, hot sagebrush hills. He said to walk north and then east following the contact of two rock formations and he would pick me up on another road in the late afternoon. All the roads went north-south or east-west, and he gave me a Brunton compass and a topographic map. I was to draw in the Morrison Formation on the map and take the angle of dip of the rocks. This was very exciting, because the Morrison Formation (about 150 million years old) was known to contain dinosaur fossils. The Brunton compass had a level bubble, so if you placed the compass on the dip slope of the rock units, you could get a fairly close number for the dip of the beds. Years later I could guess at the dip without a compass, but in the beginning I was very dumb.

So I was to walk on two sides of a square traverse and try to meet Professor Branson on the north-south road. If I couldn't find him, I could always retrace my steps—maybe.

The last thing I said was, "I have never seen a rattlesnake. How will I know one?"

Branson said, "You'll know." Then he drove off.

I wasn't exactly scared, just apprehensive, but the fact that the Morrison Formation contained remains of all sorts of dinosaurs spurred me on. I had all day to look for a skull, or a big thighbone, or a whole animal. In the beginning I just looked for gizzard stones. Some dinosaurs used small pebbles in a crop, like a chicken, to aid in digestion of plants and seeds. I found too many beautiful, polished stones, pebble-size, so I decided they couldn't all be from dinosaurs.

Then I heard this rattle, really a fast buzz, and Branson was correct, because I knew instantly that a rattlesnake was near. I acted really crazy. I crawled up on a huge boulder and yelled for help and screamed, too.

There was no one around and it was hot and my heart was beating like mad, making such a noise that I couldn't hear the snake. So I stopped yelling for fear of having a heart attack. One could dry up into a mummy in a day out there.

The snake buzzed again from under a rock, but I didn't examine its home. I didn't get much done on the field map, and I didn't find a dinosaur bone. I spent the whole day trying *not* to walk near the outcrops of rock or near boulders, because the snakes, naturally, were under everything, trying to stay out of the sun.

Just about sunset, I made it to the other road and Dr. Branson was driving up and down the road trying to find me. I told him about the snake(s). He didn't ever ask to see my map.

We had one student from the University of Chicago who was collecting rattlesnake skins for a bag and shoes. Everyone hated her. She was either too brave or too silly. She always came in with a paper shopping bag full of half-dead rattlesnakes. She just whacked them with her hammer and put them in the bag. I hope she is still alive.

Bridge Games

At the geology camp in Wyoming, most students were inking their maps at night. Observations were made with pencil in the field and then made permanent with ink at night. We were mapping simple oil domes. The domes contained oil. We knew that because they were pumping thick, black oil. Most of this oil was used for asphalt paving. Also, if you could see the structure from a distance, the beds of rock formed a "closed," elongated dome—the classic structural trap.

On the ground, with just a topographic map, a pencil, and a canteen of water, the geology seemed very difficult to me. The weather was hot and dry. There was no shade except in a few irrigation ditches that flowed through the oil structures. Grouse shared the irrigation ditches with us, and when they took off with a loud flapping of wings, we were startled. Everyone was on alert for rattlesnakes—so many rattlesnakes. It is a miracle that the students were not bitten.

Since this was the middle of World War II, there were only four men around and about twenty-five women. One girl grabbed the best guy, even though he was quite a bit younger than she. We called her the Black Widow. Consequently, there wasn't much to do at night except study or go to sleep early.

But Professor Branson was a bridge addict. He played every afternoon at the faculty club while he was on campus in Columbia, Missouri. In Wyoming, after dinner, he was at loose ends to find partners. He was anxious to play bridge every night, but he had a difficult time finding a foursome.

There was Dr. Nightingale, a professor of chemistry. I guess she was our chaperone. Then there was Mary, a graduate student and chief breakfast cook. I was Mary's assistant, so I was drafted into the foursome. I think I would like to play bridge if I had time to learn. But as a beginner, I didn't keep track of which cards had been played, and I didn't want to ask for a lot of instructions. I was playing along hoping that Dr. Branson could keep us straightened out.

Dr. Branson had his own cottage, a small cabin with

a bed, chest, and table. He ate in the dining hall with us. On one of his windowsills, he had a lineup of Nehi soda in bottles. They weren't cold, just as cool as the night air would get them. It was a beautiful array of green (lime), orange, strawberry, root beer, grape, and cream, which was clear.

Dr. Nightingale was allowed first choice, then Mary, and then I was last. That was our protocol every night that we played. Dr. Branson had two bottles of whatever pop was left.

I was Professor Branson's partner. This was a dangerous position to be in, since he gave out the final grades for the course in field geology. I tried to be very cautious in order to please him. He was a very gentle person, but during the bridge games he glared at me a lot and tapped his fingers on the table when I was trying to think.

I didn't worry about what our opponents had. I just tried to worry about our cards. Several times I was lucky enough to have good cards that I could lay down as the dummy and Branson could play. I was the all around dummy in the whole game.

Branson coached me a lot when we were in the field. He even talked about bridge when we went fishing. I couldn't fish well either, but he gave me a cane pole with about twenty feet of line and an artificial fly. In those days, even I could haul trout out of the Middle Fork of the Popo Agie River, when I didn't have the line snagged in the brush.

In one of the more exciting bridge games, someone bid three clubs and I said, "Double." I must have been drunk on orange soda pop.

Branson reached across the table and pounded it in front of me. "You never double three clubs." Why not? No one ever told me. I am still trying to figure out why he was so angry. I know we lost, but I can't remember if I doubled him or the opponents?

The other women left early, and Branson cooled down. We were trying to figure out what to do tomorrow—that is, go on a field trip to look at rocks or go fishing. Everything about this field camp was relaxing except the bridge games.

So I was about half an hour behind Mary in arriving at our cabin. Mary and I had the only cabin across the creek, and we got there by crossing a wobbly suspension bridge. The bridge was very exciting during June and July, when snow melted in the mountains and the water rose at night and lapped at the bridge.

The door was locked. Mary usually didn't do that so I pounded at the door and yelled, but I just couldn't wake her. The night was inky black. We had a huge pine tree just beyond the cabin, and I turned to rest for a while trying to figure out how to get inside. My eyes became a little accustomed to the dark, and there was a large animal slowly crawling up the tree.

My first thought was, *This is a bear and it is going to leap on me.* I called, "Marrrry," but no sound came out of my mouth. I felt as if I were screaming from a deep cave. I slid to the ground in a heap.

I don't know what finally stirred Mary, but she opened the door a crack and a little light filtered out. There I was on the ground, voiceless, and the animal was a big porcupine with all its quills bristling out so it did look very large.

Now I have learned that people do lose control of their vocal cords when scared and that porcupines often climb trees but slowly, while black bears are much faster.

Mary went to work for an oil company in Texas and became one of their chief micropaleontologists. She studied the tiny creatures in drill cores of rocks so she could tell the drillers the age and stratigraphic position of the rocks they were drilling deep underground. Perhaps she now owns the oil company, but I won't forgive her for sleeping so soundly.

Craps

Once in a while, we got to leave the geology camp and go to the town of Lander, Wyoming. It was about twelve miles east of the camp, out of the mountains, on the flat sedimentary rocks of the valley. In those bygone days, Lander was the perfect set for a western movie. It had a small two-story hotel, a bank, some stores, two gasoline stations, many saloons, and lots of dust.

There were vacant lots right on the main street, and Indians came into town and camped near the street. They were most colorful, with blankets wrapped around their shoulders. Most of the women were grouped around cooking stones, with iron pots of food boiling away.

"What do you suppose they are cooking?" I asked a white man on the street. He had new, shiny boots, but otherwise he was a mess. I should have just asked the Indians, but I was too shy. As it turned out, I am glad I didn't ask directly because I might have looked into the pots.

The man in the handsome boots said, "They are cooking their dogs." Oh, I was sorry I'd asked. I could not get this out of my mind. I wouldn't be able to eat my dog, cat, calf, pig, lamb, or whatever, if it had followed me around. All would be my friends. Now I am close to being a vegetarian. Perhaps that started in Lander.

Actually, Mary and I did have extra chances to go to town in the daytime. One day we were to pick up food, including ice cream. We could go to the creamery and choose a flavor. That day we asked for black cherry, and the man hauled out a huge metal milk can and took off the top to be sure it was black cherry. What a sight! Before the ice cream froze, the cherries rose to the top of the can—great gobs of cherries with a little ice cream matrix. We asked the creamery man to put the big can between the seats in the front of the carryall. We found an old spoon in the vehicle, and we took turns driving and eating the cherries. The rest of the students wouldn't miss all those cherries anyway.

Every other Saturday night, a carryall left camp for a night on the town. We assembled after dinner, and we had to be back by eleven at night. Since we were mostly females, we paid attention to all of the rules. If we had men along, I doubt if they would have come back until Sunday night, after a big weekend of women, drinking and hangovers.

Drinking alcohol—it seemed to me that if you were white and could lift a bottle or a glass, you could drink all the beer you could hold. No one ever asked about IDs and ages. One Saturday night we went into a saloon just to gawk at the clientele, and beyond the bar, in a back room, they had a crap table. The table was surrounded by men wildly shaking dice and yelling at each other. I stood at the edge of the table and tried to figure out the game. I had two silver dollars, but I didn't know how to shoot craps. I watched awhile. The green table was marked, field, come, pass, and had a lot of dice combinations printed on the table, such as two 3s or two 4s and

3 to 1 and the "hardway," and they were shuffling around a marker onto various numbers and patterns. The players were using silver dollars. They were real dollars, made of silver. Most of the men put one to five dollars on the "come" line.

The man next to me rolled the dice. I remember that he was left-handed and his arm brushed mine. Everyone around the table said, "Damn." The house man scooped in all the money. The player next to me rolled three—craps.

Then the house man said, "Lady coming out." He pushed the dice at me with his stick. Here we go.

I put one of the silver dollars on the come line and made nineteen passes. It was some sort of record, but each time I won, I took one dollar back. When it ended I had about twenty silver dollars and I was excited as hell. Four of the geology students were jumping up and down like children. They were back from the edge of the table. They didn't dare come too close. An old sheepherder, maybe only forty, tapped me on the shoulder and said, "Here, take these." He gave me five more silver dollars and told me he had won over two hundred dollars betting on me. I was a heroine.

Now I know how to shoot craps, but it is not as much fun. In the Lander days, everyone at the table was having fun. Nowadays, most of the players look grim and the house has three to five people watching every move. It's a police station.

Elengel

Professor Mehl, a teacher at the geology camp, often spoke about Elengel. Mehl said Elengel had been a student and instructor at our geology camp several years ago. Now he was working in the Owl Creek Mountains to the east, about ninety miles away. Sometimes we fancied that we could see the Owl Creek Mountains from the Wind River Range, when the air was very clear.

What Mehl said about this guy was that he was dirty all the time and that he lay around in the gutters of Thermopolis, Wyoming—drunk on Saturday nights. From the way Mehl pronounced the man's name, I thought he was Italian. "Elegele?" I used to pronounce it to myself. Clearly, Professor Mehl, who was with us part of the summer, didn't like that man at all. No one said the name clearly—Al Engel, two words.

Mehl said that this fellow worked alone and then went into town and "tied one on." But I thought, *If he was alone in the Owl Creek Mountains, then he was probably glad to see people when he got into town.* In 1943, this man—Elengel—was a graduate student at Princeton and he was doing a doctoral thesis, or "he was trying to do a thesis," as Professor Mehl said.

Being dirty I could understand. No one had a way to wash clothes. We washed our clothes by tying them to a rope and lowering them into the stream at night. The water pounded the clothes on stream boulders, and the next morning, they were "clean." Then we hung them on trees to dry.

Everyone in Wyoming was sweaty, dusty, and smelly, but lying around in the gutter sounded awful. However, most of the women were intrigued by this older geologist. They wanted to meet him. He didn't come to the geology camp, so we didn't see him.

When I met this fellow, at the University of Missouri campus, in Columbia, he was relatively clean and he wasn't drunk. His hair was blondish and his eyes were blue and is name was Albert Edward John Engel.

"How come you have so many names?" I asked.

"My parents named me for all of my uncles. German people used to do that to honor the family. I have a lot of relatives."

"Oh." His name was Albert Engel—Al for short.

On our first date, he took me to the Russian ballet. We saw *Swan Lake*. We were married that year (1944). He didn't drink much, but he did get drunk occasionally, particularly if the liquor was free—at geological meetings and at parties. He still has some dirty clothes. He always has three piles of clothes going at once— possible, impossible, and clothes he should throw away.

Field Trips

At the University of Missouri, everyone loved to get out of class to go on a geologic field trip. We had been on one-day trips to collect fossils and look at sedimentary rocks, but this time we were going to the TriState lead-zinc district to study the large deposits of lead and zinc ores. We would stay overnight. The TriState mines were near the junction of Missouri, Oklahoma, and Kansas.

As I look back, none of these field trips was well planned. We filed on to the old bus with a blanket and a jacket. I can't remember if we had food or where we planned to sleep. No matter, the less planning the better—sometimes. We didn't get to the mines on the first day, but I recall eating in a café somewhere in southwest Missouri. Then it started to rain, very hard. It was springtime and not too cold. Professor Branson rummaged through his pockets and billfold to find enough money for two cabins—one for the men and the other for the women. We had to chip in with what money we had. I think we all had to bring three dollars for the entire trip. We were poor.

We all spread out into two little cabins. Because each had only one bed, most of us were on the floor. I don't think we slept at all. We had breakfast at another little café and then arrived at the mine in the early morning. This was a walk-in "room and pillar" mine, having no shaft with a hoist or elevator. Huge trucks were rumbling in and out of the enormous entrance to the mine. The mine manager said we were welcome and to take our time. Two warnings: "Don't fall under the ore trucks, and don't collect samples." The latter was forbidden—no taking of samples out of the mine.

But the minerals were gorgeous. We all got off to one side where the trucks were not running and started to examine the walls of the mine workings. There were little and big cavities everywhere, partially filled with magnificent cubes of galena, lead sulfide (PbS), many with ruby-colored sphalerite crystals (ZnS) growing on the galena. We couldn't decide what to steal first. Our pockets were not big enough, so we tied strings and ropes around our ankles and started to fill up our pants, but lead sulfide is heavy. We had to hide the ropes that secured our pants in our boots and try not to look too lumpy when we came out of the mine. I could have spent a year in there picking out the very best specimens. Everything was museum grade, but the St. Joseph Lead Company was just grinding it up. They could have doubled their income selling the best quality specimens to schools, museums, and rock hounds, but this company had tunnel vision. What a shame.

This was a do-your-own-thing field trip, because Dr. Branson didn't come into the mine. He was a paleontologist and knew very little about mineral deposits, and he wasn't interested in learning about them.

When we came out, loaded with mineral specimens, we tried to look innocent. It isn't easy, weighted down with big cubes of lead sulfide. The mine captain asked us into the office to see the really fine specimens that they had saved. Even they didn't grind up the most beautiful samples. The floor of the office was wood, and we were standing around attentively when the rope on one girl's pant leg loosened—clunk. She bent down and whipped the specimen into her hat, which was in her hand. Clunk, clunk—she didn't get the rope around her jeans tightened. Well, the mine captain sort of smiled and he let us take everything we stole. I guess if he didn't have some feeble rules, people would have come in with buckets and emptied the mine.

Now, almost forty years later, the TriState lead-zinc district is one big disaster for the EPA and the poor people who live around there. When the ore was mined out, the mining companies stopped pumping out the groundwater. The whole region of mined out rock is filled to overflowing with contaminated groundwater. The groundwater has slowly reacted with the sulfides to produce sulfuric acid, which has begun to flow out on the surface of farmers' fields nearby. I read about horses in the fields with feet and hair burned by acid, and I don't know what the people in the surrounding area drink now. They have a lot of toxic heavy metals floating around in the acid groundwater and no simple or economical way to solve the problem. At last count, the EPA had hundreds of toxic mine dumps and mines filled with heavy metals—arsenic, lead, cadmium, and others, which are floating around in the drinking water and blowing around in the air we breathe. And they don't have enough money or clear-cut solutions in sight to clean up the gigantic messes that we have made.

Another memorable field trip in my senior year was a climb to the top of Wind River Peak in Wyoming. This trip was to be the climax of a summer of field studies in geology. We started from Camp Lander at seven thousand feet and walked about twelve miles to a camp at the base of the peak. Wind River Peak is about 13,400 feet high. We had horses carrying bedrolls and food and cooking utensils and a stove. My dear mother sent me a new pair of boots, and they seemed to fit. She also sent red wool socks. I know she had the very best intentions, and I was too young to worry about my feet.

Professor Mehl was our guide. He rode a horse while we trudged up the winding trail. In any group like this, there are the strong walkers and the weak ones. It was 1943 and we didn't have but three guys along. Some of the women could have climbed Mount Everest. As it turned out, I was one of the weaker members of the party—a tenderfoot.

This trail to Bill's Lake at the base of the peak was well worn. It passed through several meadows where the stream meandered around in tall grass. Mosquitoes rose out of the meadows by the millions. Three of us, all women, decided to walk one behind the other, close together. Each was responsible for chasing mosquitoes off the neck and head of the person ahead. The person in back was without protection, so we rotated from the rear to the front. Still we were all bitten and full of welts. What did those mosquitoes eat when we were not there? Game animals and cattle that wandered into the national forest? We had thinner skin and they dined on us night and day.

My feet began to hurt. The boots were too new and stiff, and the red color of the socks faded into my new blisters. I was the last one into base camp, dead tired and with bad feet. That night we all slept around the fire, as close as we could get, because the mosquitoes stayed away from the fire. A burning cinder from the campfire flew into one eye. *Now I will be blind, too,* I thought.

The next day, all of the rest of the students started out to climb Wind River Peak. They were gone all day. I rested and soaked my feet. The weather was hot in the daytime and cold at night. But the campsite was truly beautiful, with the lake at our feet and the peak gleaming in the sunlight. I looked at it all, lying down. Professor Mehl stayed in camp, too. He wasn't a mountain man.

Then the hikers started dribbling back into camp. All but two of them gave up along the way up. It was another ten miles round trip. They stayed in pairs, on the buddy system. A girl from the University of Chicago (the rattlesnake woman) and a skinny guy managed to get to the top of Wind River Peak and add their names to the list in a can at the top. She was the daughter of a geologist and mountain climber and had climbed most of the high mountains in Wyoming. The guy was wiry and small. They said he was too small to be in the army.

They put my boots with the bedrolls on one of the

horses, and we all started back down the trail to Camp Lander. Each person who could spare a pair of socks gave them to me. I wore four layers of socks and no shoes and managed to hobble twelve miles back to camp. It was all downhill. At first, I went slowly, and of course, I was alone. Then I began to worry about meeting a bear so I hurried faster. How come they didn't put me on a horse? You really should not leave one of your tenderfoot students behind. I sang, yelled, and whistled. There were huge boulders in the trail, and I imagined coming face to face with a bear on the other side of a boulder. But I didn't see a thing.

Years later, when Al and I had two young sons, we went back to the Wind River Mountains to fish. Al and the younger son, Tom, were the fishermen. Bob, our older son, and I decided to take the trail back to our rented car and go into town to shop at Lander, Wyoming. On the way out, I tripped on a root in the trail and fell down—plop—the sort of fall that is so fast that your brain doesn't even get a warning.

Bob said, "Mom, are you all right?"

"Yes, I guess."

We finally arrived at Lander. We bought some peaches and apples and were carrying them in paper bags. The peaches smelled good. The trail back to the fishing camp went through an area of forest so thick that nothing grew on the ground. It was dark in there. I was watching for exposed roots. Bob was ahead and he turned to me and said, "Mom, if a bear comes along and wants those peaches, you are going to give them to him, aren't you?"

"Yes, if we see a bear I am going to throw all of the fruit as far as I can in the direction of the bear. Okay?"

"Yes, I was hoping you wouldn't try to hang onto the peaches."

He thought I was clumsy and crazy.

Well, I was crazy. I let the boys bring back two garter snakes to California. Each son had one snake in a paper bag. We were traveling by train, and on the last leg to Los Angeles we were in coach. The snakes kept peaking out of the paper bags. The snakes arrived safely, but what if one had managed to escape in a crowded railroad car? Passengers would have panicked.

Then there were the field trips in our research areas in succeeding years. During our work in the northwest Adirondack Mountains, in New York, we had a lot of visitors, both foreign geologists and groups out of the big labs, like the Geophysical Laboratory of the Carnegie Institution in Washington, D.C. Al was always excited when these geological groups arrived. He wanted to show them everything—instantly. I went along on many of these trips. These groups included the big names in the earth sciences, both field geologists and laboratory people. Through the early years, I remember only one woman, and she was tough as nails.

These trips involved a lot of people in cars. There was not much walking, in order to save time and cover much more of the region. One day we came to a rock complex that Al wanted to explain in detail. Also, he liked to whip up a good argument. A few of the hardbitten geologists paid attention, but all of the lab men were crawling around on the ground eating wild strawberries. Golly, they were good and there were a lot of them. The sun was out and it was warm, and all they wanted to do was lean up against outcrops of rock and eat strawberries. Finally, all the geologists were on the ground, too, eating strawberries.

Al said, "They aren't listening to me."

I said, "Oh, let them eat strawberries. Most of them

are along for a sort of vacation, a picnic. They don't want to listen to you all day long." Al gave up, but he was miffed about it. These were his rocks and he thought he had a fascinating story to tell, but the rocks were no match for the wild strawberries.

I saw a little of this intensity for teaching in our older son. One year he brought a group of botanists to Montana. The participants ranged in age from sixteen to sixty-seven. One day Bob had them climb an enormous mountain in order to study plants as they survived in dwarf form at timberline. At night they were all exhausted, but Bob was going to drag out a blackboard to explain orographic barriers and weather.

I pleaded, "Stop, don't talk. They are tired and need to rest their legs and brains." He listened to me but he hated to quit. It is true that "the apple does not fall far from the tree."

The last big field trip I went on was my last. The Geological Society of America was meeting in Denver, Colorado, in November. It was unseasonably cold. Before the meetings they were to have a field trip led by the local guys into the mountains. We both signed up to go, or more probably, Al signed me up when he signed up. So we all clambered onto buses at 8:00 A.M. They always start at eight in the morning, which is a terrible time to be dressed and cheerful. And they don't quit until it is too dark to see the rocks.

The bus headed west from Denver into the mountains. Snow was blowing all over the place. It was biting cold and with the wind, the chill factor was zero. The first stop was at an exposure of banded gneiss—you don't care what that is—and they swept snow off the outcrop. I got out and looked at it. Okay, I have seen a lot of banded gneisses, so I got back on the bus. The motor was running so the heater was on in the bus. I didn't care if I was the first one to quit. The bus drove higher into the mountains—more banded gneisses and more cold and wind. At the last stop, most of the geologists were huddled in a drafty shaft house of an abandoned mine to discuss and argue. I got back on the bus. The other woman gave up, too. The head of the Geophysical Lab was the first man back on the bus; then they started to get back on the bus in droves. Al and the field trip leader were last to get on the bus. They were still talking about banded gneisses.

Talc Mines

Albert and I were married in Washington, D.C., in June 1944, and we stayed in the city for several weeks, during World War II. The city was hot, humid, and crowded, and everyone was working very hard for the war effort. Long lines of people were forming everywhere, for buses and food. Many of us worked far into the night. We had a partial blackout, particularly of government buildings and memorials. Trains were packed with soldiers coming and going.

I was just learning to type. A lot of our reports had to be done in a big hurry. There was a furious hunt going on for strategic minerals. The U.S. needed just about everything but enthusiasm. My husband was deferred for the moment from military service, and he was going to be sent to Brazil, they said, to evaluate deposits of quartz crystals needed for radio sets. Later they made good synthetic quartz crystals. Transistor radio equipment was way off in the distant future. Albert was stuck full of shots, which made him ill, but he was ready to go to Brazil.

I had a nonproblem. I tried to stay well dressed, with a suit or dress and high-heeled shoes, and my feet were killing me. It is crazy to be that vain. Then my husband's orders were canceled. He was to go to all the talc mines in Vermont and New York State to map the mines and try to get production of talc stepped up. That talc was not for face powder. It was for marking welding points, for vulcanizing rubber, and for the matrix in battleship paint. Talc was another strategic mineral. It was truly amazing that the United States didn't know much about its resources or those of its allies. We have used up most of our resources in World War II, Korea, and Vietnam, and now we are a resource-poor nation.

Al and I were able to check out a typewriter and a petrographic microscope. With our clothes and a few wedding presents, we were able to carry everything we owned in two suitcases.

Out of New York City, we boarded a coach on the Boston and Maine Railroad. The windows were open and the black ash from the coal-fired engine poured through the windows. It was hot. Somewhere near Hanover, New Hampshire, we got off and were met by the chief of our section. My husband always apologized to everyone because I was along with him. Wives did not go into the field with their husbands, because there were only a few women who were geologists or even interested in geology. Some field parties considered women bad luck. Yes, it was the dark ages.

The strategic minerals group gave us a U.S. Government car, a black Ford. It was one of the last sedans made for other than military use. It had a governor on the accelerator so that we could not go faster than thirty-five miles per hour. Everyone was supposed to drive slowly to save gasoline and tires, but it was difficult to go up hills or pass anything with that block on the accelerator.

The black Ford didn't have a heater. Are you saying, "Tough luck?" It was twenty to thirty degrees below zero Fahrenheit on many winter mornings at five-thirty when we went to work. The mines were forty-five degrees above zero, and on cold mornings, we were happy to go underground.

We went first to the Mad River talc mine in Vermont. This mine produced talc pencil stock. This material was a very fine-grained talcose rock that was sawed into rectangular, thin pencils. Talc pencil stock was used to mark weld sites on ships, and it will not melt off in the heat of a welding torch. We needed talc pencil stock badly. However, this mine had been abandoned some years before and it was filled with water. I think they had mined out most of the good stuff but were trying to reopen during the war. A lot of mines that were closed or largely worked out were reopened during World War II.

The mine operator was a cheerful, optimistic fellow anxious to show us everything. He had a tall stepladder propped up against the walls of the shaft, and that is the way we crawled down to the first level. Below was the near-vertical shaft to deeper levels, all filled with water.

Ordinary light bulbs were strung along a wire as far down as we could see in the mine. The amazing thing is that these lights were burning underwater. The owner was trying to pump out the water so they could work the mine again. Most talc mines in the east are very wet, but not this wet. This mine was a disaster.

I was frightened—no, scared to death—about going farther into the mine, with its deadly combination of water and electricity, but my husband glared at me, so I didn't make a commotion. The mine owner asked us to follow him on an underground goat trail so narrow that we had to face the mine wall and creep along a narrow ledge into the pump room. I didn't want to see the pumps, I just wanted to get out of there. What if we fell off the ladder into the chasm of electrified water? The mine operator went first, then my husband, and he did say not to look down, so I hugged the wall with both arms outstretched and hit all the bare wires and felt the electricity run through every part of my body. I was lucky, I guess. After that, I hurried the rest of the way. On the way back, I didn't touch a thing except bare rock and that with only my index fingers. It is insane to go into mines filled with water and electricity. Any fool knows that.

Much true talc occurs as greasy, flaky crystals that just smear around and are difficult to grind up into small particles. What the mines called talc was really a combination of talc flakes, fibers, asbestos, serpentine, tremolite, anthophylite, some calcium carbonate, and any other junk they can find that will grind up to a near-white color. They couldn't use too much calcium carbonate or it would react with other substances in the liquid in paint and insecticide or if heated.

With all the fibrous minerals that are mined, the miners and mill operators die of lung diseases (fibrosis, silicosis, cancer, and emphysema). When we were in the mines, they were drilling dry—that is, without water at the drill points—and the air was full of fibers. We could see the fibers floating in the air in the light beam attached to our hard hats. No one wore filter masks. We were stupid, too, just for working in these mines. We were too young then to worry about dying of cancer or emphysema. Besides, we had to win the war.

We don't know if they were ever able to get the water

out of the Mad River talc mine, but the mines in upstate New York were open and working. My husband was sent there to evaluate the "talc" ore for use in the war effort.

The main talc zone from Balmat to Edwards, New York, consisted of zones and lenses that thickened and thinned along its length of about twelve miles. There were five separate mines along the thicker, purer parts of the talc zone and lots of prospect holes. Each mine had a shaft, headframe, and hoist. Each mine was supposed to have two shafts, one called "a second way out." It is just what the names implies, another way to get to the surface in case of a major cave-in or other disaster. In all of our mapping underground, we never found a second exit. Miners and ore went up and down the only shaft in a skip. The skip was a large rectangular bucket with wheels that rode on narrow rails. The skip was pulled up and down by a cable operated from the hoist house.

The skip was as slippery as ice, because the minerals were both slippery and wet. The skip was operated from the hoist house with a bell system—two bells for men in the skip and one bell if ore was in the skip. Naturally, the hoist man ran the skip more carefully if miners were in the skip. If he had a load of ore, then it was slam, bang, get to the surface, dump the ore, and lower away for another load.

One mine had a particularly exciting ride to the bottom, because the shaft was dug along the commercial talc zone. Near the surface the talc zone was almost flat, so we started down in the skip lying on our backs. Then, as the talc zone steepened, the skip rolled over, still riding on the iron rails, and we finally arrived at the bottom of the mine in a near-vertical position. It was similar to a ride down one side of a roller-coaster, but more slowly.

At the bottom, I was always scrambling and clawing to get out of the skip. I tried to remain composed and professional, but I was forever slipping back and floundering around in the skip. My husband always had to pull me out. Otherwise, I would have ended up under the next load of ore—crushed.

Since the man in the hoist house rarely saw the skip, he had to paint marks on the cable, which wound out of a huge drum. He used a different color for the depth of successive mine levels. He couldn't see the miners in the skip either. I always hoped that the hoist operator had heard the two bells for "men on."

They didn't waste much time. The next car of ore was ready at the skip the moment we got out.

Then Al decided it was necessary to map the form and structure of the talc zone on levels that were worked out—that is, abandoned forever. In this case, Al had to signal when we reached the first or second level by grabbing out for a rope, which in some cases wasn't there. Also, the hoist operator had to guess how much cable to let out to get to an abandoned level because the paint marks on the cable were worn off. Sometimes we were too low or too high in the shaft. We had to scramble out and crawl along next to the tracks.

The cable that pulled the skip had some spring in it, so the skip bobbed up and down several feet before it came to rest. We were on a big yo-yo. However, this happened only when we were trying to get off on the abandoned levels. Most abandoned levels had a sawbuck at the entrance with a crudely printed sign labeled, "Danger, Keep Out."

The first abandoned level we worked in was very spooky. If we were quiet for a minute, we could hear rock falling and water dripping from the ceilings. We did a lot of stupid things, but most of the mines had no maps at all. For example, they didn't know if they were mining out pillars that held up the overlying rock because they had no maps of the abandoned levels or of the ceilings and sides of the enlarged mined-out areas, called stopes. The falling rock in the abandoned levels was "working," as the miners called it. Also, while working on the first level, we could occasionally see daylight through cracks in the ceiling. That was very distressing, because there was nothing holding up the ceiling.

One day at lunchtime, we were sitting on a pile of rock that had fallen from the ceiling. We had some sort of miserable lunch in bags. When we finished, Al went back to the surveyor's instrument he had set up in an abandoned drift, and the next thing I heard was a tremendous crash of more rock falling from the ceiling. It really sounded so close that Al might be under it. But he was okay. The ceiling had caved in and fallen next to him. He was looking pale and examining the instrument to find out if it was damaged. We continued working, but I knew for sure that we were both crazy.

We mapped what we could of mine workings and then tied that data to the surface. In the search for the best talc, we found two of the mines were across their boundaries, well into other companies' land or claim.

One mine, called the Ontario, was mining under a major river. Seventeen feet separated the upper mine level from the bottom of the river gravels. Al and I used to joke together that if we saw the river dry up in a hurry, then it went into the Ontario mine. Another mine was working under a lake. We could feel the 3:30 P.M. blasts of dynamite under our lakeside cabin.

We were in and near the talc mines for five years.

When I look at a container of powdered insecticide and read the label, which states 94 percent are "inert" ingredients, I know where these inert materials came from. A lot of the inert materials are from these talc mines. And there are a lot of inert miners who died from the dust in those mines.

Minerals

When we went to Vermont, Al's third job assignment after studies of domestic supplies of manganese and quartz crystals, our objective was to evaluate crayon and other talcs for the U.S. Navy.

We did have a petrographic microscope, but I didn't know how to use it. We were living in a shack near Stowe, Vermont. Our house was one of the tiny cabins in a tourist camp. Later, we were able to have what used to be the office and cafe, and that was larger. They had neglected to take down the cafe sign, and a few truck drivers stopped in to ask, "What's for lunch?" "This isn't a cafe anymore, sorry," I replied. Behind the cabins was an acre plot of red raspberries. We ate a lot of raspberries while thousands of poor soldiers ate Spam. I made a lot of preserves and jelly.

Now I was crabbing around a lot about what to do all day. The locals, the Yankees of Vermont, were unfriendly. Many of the local men had been drafted, and some women resented the fact that Al had not been drafted. He was deferred to do national resource work.

"Well, get out the microscope and learn how to identify minerals." Al said to me. "Here are two books for you to read."

One book was about how to operate the microscope, and the other contained data on the optical properties of minerals. Through the years I guarded the optical properties of minerals book as if it was the family Bible. It was all dog-eared and stained, and I hung onto it for thirty years. It contained the optical constants of all minerals, and it opened up a whole new world for me.

Al ground up a mineral for me and said to identify it before he came out of the mine at night. Since I couldn't work in the talc mines of Vermont—Al had an assistant, and only two outside people could go into the mines at one time—I set up the microscope. We had blank slides, immersion oils for determining indices of refraction of minerals, cover glasses, an agate mortar and pestle, a tiny spatula, and other odds and ends. I had the mineral powder that Al prepared in a small envelope.

It took me all day and a lot of sweating to identify the mineral. It was quartz, silicon dioxide, one of the common minerals in the crust of the earth, perhaps the most common mineral.

I liked this microscope work on mineral particles. Give me a powdered mineral, and I could work out its optical properties and accurately identify it. I ran around like mad in the morning—washing dishes, sweeping, and picking raspberries—in order to get back to the microscope. Then I worked on the feldspars, which are K-Na-Al silicates. A petrographic microscope has plain or polarized light in which to study optical properties of minerals. No two minerals are alike. In polarized light many minerals have distinctive rainbowlike colors, but some minerals are dark in polarized light. These are isotropic minerals and no matter how you rotate the minerals, light is coming through at the same velocity. I learned that much later. I didn't have a lot of exotic minerals at the beginning except when we started looking at many uncommon fine-grained minerals from the talc mines. The microscope was a powerful tool in identifying these minerals.

When I was given some of these exotic industrial minerals to identify, that was much more taxing, and I was getting to be an expert in optical mineralogy and wouldn't let anyone touch "my" microscope.

Much later we also had thin sections of rocks, talc rock, marbles, metamorphosed granitic rocks, and schists and gneisses. The thin sections were prepared in Washington, D.C., by the U.S. Geological Survey and sent back to us. Working out the mineralogy and texture of these rocks showed me minute segments of our planet that few people ever see. And they told an amazing story of the geological history of the region. I did less cleaning and cooking, and we didn't have as many raspberries. But one day while I was picking, a young woman across the row asked about Al. She complained that her husband was drafted and in the army. Well, everyone can't be in the army, some men had to do other things, like work in mines to find and evaluate the important minerals needed for war. About this time, Al was offered a position with the army signal corps. He would have been an officer in uniform, and I would not have had to explain him away.

If someone asked Al why he was deferred, he said, "I am a single man with children." People puzzled over that. That was funny in 1944, but now there are a lot of single men with children.

After the first summer in the raspberry patch in Vermont, we moved to the mines of upstate New York.

The chief of the section said we would be there "until the snow flies." We were there through five years. I had some of the same minerals in these deposits, but I found many new ones with the aid of the microscope and the tattered book of optics. I became so dependent on the microscope that I wouldn't try to identify a mineral without my microscope. Then, near the end of World War II, Al was drafted. But they found they didn't need him anymore. He was getting too old.

We decided to try to work together at a university. After checking out a lot of schools, we decided to go to Caltech in Pasadena, California. Everyone was going to California.

I thought that I knew just about every common mineral and many not-so-common varieties. We started crushing the major rock types from the talc-producing districts of New York. We sieved the crushed samples and separated minerals for chemical analyses, optical properties, and X-ray studies.

I don't care how one plans—there are always gaps in the data. We often had too much rock from one area and not enough of an exciting mineral from another. We used heavy liquids, bromoform and methylene iodide to make a rough mineral separation and then refined the separation on a magnetic separator. It took months and months to achieve these mineral separations, but I have finished it in a paragraph. In addition, the heavy liquids were carcinogenic.

Our plan was to study the variations in properties of each mineral as it formed under different conditions of temperature and pressure.

We had bottles and bottles of garnet, amphiboles, and biotite (Fe-Mg-Al silicates). Some mineral separates were almost too small to analyze at the time—weighing less than three grams—but most were larger. Also, we had the granddaddy sample, a big sample, fifteen grams or more of two very distinctive biotites. One type came from a rock formation formed at moderate temperatures and pressures. The other came from the same formation reconstituted at higher temperatures and pressures much deeper in the earth. We wanted to carefully document the changes in the mineral in these two very different earth environments. One biotite was red and titanium-rich and represented the high-temperature, high-pressure environment. The other was greenish brown, and I had them as pure as we could get them. Each sample formed a good-sized pile on the big filter paper. It was the last separation through one of the heavy liquids, and they were washed with acetone and dried. I was pleased and I went to get Al to show him. I think Bill Otto was with us, too.

We three sat at the end of the table in the laboratory and gloated over the large size and purity of the samples and all of the data we were going to get from the minerals. Then I did an insane thing. I picked up the one filter paper with the red biotite and poured it into the other—mixing the samples and ruining all the work. I can't imagine what happened to me. Lost my mind? Mental fatigue? Pilot error? Crazy? I had poured so many mineral separations off filter papers that I did it one more time at the very worst time, in the wrong direction, with a critical set of samples.

I was crying all over the place, and tears rained into the mixed-up minerals. The two men were very gentle. They just patted me and said it was okay. "Don't be upset," they said. "You didn't mean to do it." If they had yelled at me, I would have had to be carried away in a strait jacket.

I know that other scientists make mistakes, blunders, horrible errors, but they may not tell us about them. I just did. I have recovered from it now—thirty years later.

Natural Bridge

As work progressed on mapping the talc deposits, we went to look at another producing mine about thirty miles from the main talc zone. On route to the mine, we passed through a part of a military base, at Camp Drum, New York. It was winter and the men were learning how to fight in snow and ice. Some were on skis in white uniforms, and others were trying, unsuccessfully, to get U.S. tanks to operate in the bitter cold. A lot of soldiers were standing around discarded oil drums with fires in them, trying to keep their hands and faces warm.

I think it was a secret training base. Were we going to send troops to the Soviet Union? We couldn't think of other places in Europe where our men would have to endure winter conditions similar to these in northern New York State, except, perhaps, in Norway.

I complained that our black Ford didn't have a heater, so I stuck my feet under Al while he was driving. When we arrived at the mine, I put my boots back on. Most winter days were so cold in the early morning that it was a relief to get into the mine. The warm air of the mine came out in clouds of frozen fog. Underground, the temperature was about the same in all of the talc mines, about forty-five degrees fahrenheit all year.

The mine at Natural Bridge was probably the most dangerous mine of all. It was in a rounded pod of marble that dipped steeply into the earth. The "talc" and serpentine formed when warm mineralized fluids rose through the crackled marble pod and altered most of the rock to hydrated magnesium silicates. The mine was a maze of slippery, huge faulted blocks, some rounded and others in giant sheets. When we looked at the ceilings of the various levels in the mine, we saw great slabs of talcose rock partially cracked and ready to fall on the floor at any time. Don't look up at the ceiling—ever. This mine had two men called scalers. They were supposed to spend all of their time prying off loose blocks and slabs to keep the other miners safe.

The Natural Bridge Mine, as it was called, was one of the last to use carbide lights on the hard hats. All the other mines used electric lamps with a battery pack attached to a belt at the waist. You have to remember to take care of your own carbide lamp. Chunks of calcium carbide were put in one section of the lamp and water in the other. The water tank was rigged to allow drops of water to combine with the carbide, and the result was acetylene gas. When you light the gas, you have a good, hissing flame on the reflector of your hard hat. Then you can see all over. Most miners refurbished their lamps at lunchtime. The miners had a little shack underground for a lunchroom with a kerosene heater to take the damp chill out of the air. They told a lot of stories. I was always a sucker for more stories. One told about the time that he lighted the dynamite fuses at the head wall where they would work in the morning and then he turned and slipped on a pile of rock. When he fell, his lamp went out. He crawled as fast as he could away from the sizzling dynamite fuses. He escaped with ruptured eardrums.

Another miner fell from one level to a lower level and impaled himself on a six-foot pry bar. He survived, but he was a mess for years.

We had a funny guy who came to work each day with a piece of pie to sell. No one would buy, so he usually gave the pie away, sometimes to me.

Mines are black, not dark. You have never been in

the dark until you have been underground in an abandoned mine.

We didn't take care of our carbide lamps properly. We would work along in an abandoned level, measuring and recording rock types and structures on our map, until we both realized we couldn't see anymore. STOP. Hurry to refill one lamp before the other fades. One time both our lamps went out, but we had matches, carbide, and lots of water.

Al said, "Look how dark it is. Where are you?"

"I'm here, right next to you." Did he think I would wander off in this darkness?

I struck about a hundered matches while Al refilled both lamps, and we were off again.

Since the miners had carbide lamps and the flame leaves a big black mark on the walls, they had decorated the walls of the drifts into a porno palace. The graffiti was everywhere and very explicit. We went into this mine on Thursday or Friday and I didn't want to stare at the drawings, but I did peek sideways from under my hard hat when I thought no one was looking.

We had to talk to the mine captain about me, a female, being underground. Some miners are superstitious about having a woman working in their mine, but I didn't run into that anywhere. Still, we felt that we should ask.

When we returned to work on the following Monday, I was prepared to look at all the drawings on the walls—but they were gone! During the weekend, they had a crew come in to hose down all the walls and that was a lot of work. The only things left were a few black smudges or an odd pipe sticking out of the wall here and there. What a disappointment. I should have been able to look at everything before they erased it all. Then, too, I felt badly that the miners thought they had to erase their art because of me.

The fifth and sixth levels were the working levels of the mine at Natural Bridge, and most of the active mining was going on at the deepest level, the sixth level. Usually, they mined and drilled all day, and then near quitting time, they filled the drill holes with dynamite. Most of the miners, except the fuse men, get out before the dynamite is lighted.

We were not paying attention to time, I guess, and we were walking out of an adit (drift, tunnel, whatever) when a miner came screaming at us, "Get back, get back!" I pay strict attention to a guy who is that agitated, so we rushed back as deep as we could go into a short adit. Then the dynamite went off. It isn't just your ears that hurt like hell, or your head, but your stomach vibrates like a big drum. They had set the charges for the day in an adit that entered into ours at an angle. So we didn't get the full blast, but it was very nasty.

The miner said that he didn't know we were there. After that experience, we tried to let them know where we planned to work and we got out of the mine on time.

Geologists carry hammers that are square on one side and have a sharp pick on the other. I think they should do away with both ends. I would hate to count how many times I have taken a swing at a big boulder of talc, missed it, and hit my leg on the shinbone. Oh, the oaths and swearing and how it hurts, but you can't admit to anyone that you have just battered your leg with your hammer. It's clumsy, stupid, and unprofessional.

Also, if you want a sample from the ceiling of a mine, even though you should not mess around with the ceiling, remember that water can drop from the roof onto your face. Your brain reacts and draws your arm back, and you hit yourself in the forehead with the pick end. Perhaps I should not carry a geologic hammer? Now that it is too late, I have decided not to carry a hammer, ever.

A lot of accidents happen to talc miners. They get careless. One young man sheared off his head riding in a mine car. He didn't duck at a low spot. A lot of miners are missing fingers. Some fell through "grizzlies" and cut themselves all over. However, the greatest danger are the fibers that they breathe into their lungs. I hope they drill wet and use masks now.

All the "talc" minerals are white or pale gray and covered with gummy wet dust, but one wall in this mine was an exposure of dark serpentine with a lot of exotic minerals. Naturally, they didn't want to get near the dark rock—it would discolor the product—but I went to look at this hanging wall a lot. It contained big crystals of celestite (blue), prehnite (pink), and some other lovely minerals, which I collected. Through the years, I gave them away or lost them moving or our children took them to school to show and tell and we lost them all.

Pumpkins

We went into town, Gouverneur, New York, one Halloween to see the children in the annual parade. Many were dressed as ghosts and witches, but some were dressed as little pumpkins. I thought those little pumpkins were adorable. Next July we had a little boy pumpkin.

There was one doctor in town. He had just returned from World War II, in Europe. Office visits cost three dollars, and he had his own pharmacy. If you needed some sort of medication, he supplied it. It was included in the price of the office visit.

This man, Dr. Head, was very shy. He rarely talked, but I decided that I wanted him to talk to me.

"I am sort of afraid about having a baby," I said.

"So am I," he said.

"Why?" I was very nervous now.

"I have never delivered a baby."

Then he mumbled that there was another baby due about one month before ours. *He is going to practice on us,* I thought. He was about thirty-eight years old.

I thought briefly about going to a larger town, but it was forty miles away.

The doctor gave me two huge books, one on gynecology and the other on human embryology. I have been thinking through the years, *should he have given me those books?* Both books were filled with horror tales—the worst case possibilities. One book illustrated high forceps deliveries, babies with deformed heads, and how to crush the fetus and take it apart if deformed, and the illustrations and texts went into Siamese twins, breech deliveries, deformed babies, how and why the mother dies, and on and on.

If I had read the books before I became pregnant, we would not have had a little pumpkin. However, Dr. Head must have thought that I could handle all this information. When I tried to show some illustrations to Al, he said, "I don't want to see that."

Al had the idea that a pregnant female should lead a supernormal life. He had me walking, walking, walking. When the first pains started, he took me for a long walk—"to shake it loose," he said.

It worked. Dr. Head said that "the baby was born with the speed of an express train." That was about the longest sentence Dr. Head ever uttered.

The price was reasonable, sixty-five dollars for pre-

and post-delivery and care for the newborn. The hospital was an old house converted into a hospital. The hospital charged sixty dollars. In those bygone days, they kept you in the hospital for ten days. I was very weak and almost dead by the time I arrived home.

Now I was nailed down with the baby, but I could work between diaper changes and whatever with my microscope. And I did some drafting for Al of mine workings and surface topographic details. We had a Leroy lettering set, and I used that, too. I thought the maps I drafted were handsome, except for small smudges and wiggly lines here and there.

Our rented house was so cold in the winter that baby Bobby slept in his snowsuit and cap. A glass of water beside his bed froze almost every night. We tried to use the coal furnace and almost burned down the house. Where the furnace pipe went through the second floor, the wood floors were charred.

We were going to have just one child, but another son appeared three years later. This second boy was born midway between coasts. We lived in California, worked summers in New York State, and were returning to California when the second boy was born in Saint Louis. My mother and grandmother were delighted to have a three-year-old and a new baby to fuss over.

Al and I were lucky and unlucky with our sons. The older developed leukemia in his midthirties. The younger son turned out to be a near-perfect match for a bone-marrow transplant—almost an identical twin. Three years after that dreadful experience, we are all alive, but I am afraid to hear the telephone ring. Leukemia will never be erased from my thoughts.

Many people upwind from Chernobyl, in the Ukraine, will be ill with leukemia. Some will get sick immediately, and others will drift on for years and then become ill.

Also, we aren't certain how many cases will develop around Three-Mile Island. When I think that we put four reactors astride a major river in the eastern part of the United States, I wonder what idiot chose that site. Of course, Three-Mile Island released very little radiation compared to Chernobyl.

Many times I think that both of our sons were irradiated when we worked in Utah, upwind from all the atomic bomb tests in Nevada in the 1950s. We camped out in the open in that red dust of Utah, which was probably hot as a firecracker. However, the U.S. Government stonewalled on all of the cases of leukemia in Utah, Arizona, and Nevada, and they are just now starting to admit to anything—even that nuclear bombs were detonated.

Swamps

After we spent winter working underground in the talc mines, spring came and six feet of snow melted. Al started to map on the surface in order to project the talc deposists beyond the mine workings and, of course, to understand the regional geology and look for other mineral deposits.

Spring is very windy in upstate New York. The wind comes out of Canada, picks up speed on Lake Erie, and then just blows and blows. Al came home a lot of days all upset because the wind tore up his field maps and notebook. He was trying to write down observations, and the map sheets and the pages of the notebook flapped about in the wind.

Then summer came, usually humid and hot, with enormous numbers of insects. There were also a lot of thunderstorms and wild rainstorms.

By now, Al was mapping "quadrangles"—that is, geologic maps superimposed on topographic maps. He loved to do the exciting parts where there were lots of rocks exposed and interesting geology, but if you have to finish a quadrangle, you have to get out into the corners of the topographic maps. He hated to fill out the corners, particularly when the corners were in swamps or dull rock types. Some days I went along to learn mapping methods. The whole region was full of swamps, and we had to cross them on foot, naturally. I thought of quicksand, which was nonexistent, but I made a practice of following Al so closely as to be certain that I stepped into or near his footprints. In many places we were up to our waists in mucky water. A lot of these swamps were in thickets or scrub timber.

Black flies like to bite around the back of the ears, and I was poisoned by them. My ears swelled up and stood straight out. What a mess. Al did not get a bad reaction from insect bites, or maybe they didn't bite him. If you survive in the swamps of upstate New York, you have to be insect-resistant.

The discomfort index was high, the weather hot, and the humidity high. If you just moved around, sweat poured off your hair and face and dripped down your nose onto the map. I sweat more than Al does, so he learned not to let me check the map except from a distance of several feet. He was always in charge of the map. Of course, he knew what he was doing and I was learning.

When Al and I were newly married, we spent a weekend at Princeton, Al's graduate school, and sat on a porch under a big umbrella and drank Cokes. I remember thinking, *Now this is the life.* I was so naive that I had already forgotten the heat and snakes in Wyoming field geology classes. Somehow I thought working in the east was going to be more dressy, more mannerly, maybe just sitting under an umbrella and drinking Cokes and beer. . . .

Most of the early farming people in upstate New York raised milk cows, but the farms were too small, the soil too lean, rocky, and uneconomic, and the region too cold in winter. Much of the land was reverting to thick scrub growth. However, some farmers still had milk cows, and I do remember the Ayrshire cows. They are supposed to be milk cows, but I can't understand how anyone can catch them to milk them.

Al said, "We are going to have to cross this pasture, and it is full of Ayrshires. Get under the fence on the other side. These cows can run like hell. They have nasty horns and they will chase us."

Al could jump the fences near the fence posts, but I had to find a place to crawl under.

I always tried to look up and down the pasture to see if the beasts were in sight. Ayrshire cows have huge curled horns, and probably they could hear or smell us, because they came charging along like bulls in a ring, and these were only cows. I guess the faster I ran, the more they thought, *Let's get her.* I barely made the other fence and went scrambling under the last strand of wire. What kept the cows from just trampling through the fence? Habit, I guess. They were strong enough to level the fences.

In the fall, we worked in several places where farmers kept huge Belgian or Clydesdale horses. Everyone writes that they are gentle giants. Horse manure. They would attack us and stand up on their back legs and paw the air. Al always said, "They won't hurt you, they are just playing." I don't want to play with a ton of horse.

I have always loved dogs, but the northwest Adirondack farmers keep mean dogs. Al would have to go to the front door of a farmhouse and ask if we could work in and around the farm. When he was at the door, a dog would come creeping around from the side and nail him in the leg or ankle. Al's boots saved him from a lot of bad bites. I never offered to go to a farmhouse for anything.

We had a visitor from New Zealand, and I tagged along on that excursion, too. We had to cross a swampy pasture. The ground had big holes and high tufts where the horses and cows had sunk in as they walked. I slipped off one tuft and fell into a hole, and my ankle twisted outward with a sharp pain and a crack as if something broke. However, it didn't hurt much so I hobbled along. I was always last anyway. We sat down for lunch, and then I looked at my foot. It was huge, swollen to the size of an elephant foot.

Al said, "Don't ruin the day. Take the car and go into the hospital for an X ray, but be sure to pick us up close to this spot about 5:00 P.M."

You see, he didn't spoil me.

Death Valley

In 1948, Al and I were going west to work in California. We wanted to buy a car, a new car, because we had never had a new car. After World War II, war production slowed and companies began to produce new automobiles.

In this little upstate New York town of Gouverneur, a new Studebaker agency opened. It is too kind to call this an agency, giving some legitimacy to the operation. The guy who had the automobiles was a black market scoundrel.

The salesman let us see what he had locked up in a warehouse, and we fell for a little bright red car, a two-door with overdrive. He would not tell us the price of the car. He was going to sell it for the highest price he could get. Al visited him daily. Sometimes we went together to talk with the owner, hoping that we could charm him into selling the red car to us. After weeks of sweating over it, he finally sold us the car, and now I can't remember the price.

Al was so proud that he even washed the car once, but from that day to this (1987) I don't think he washed another car.

So we dropped off our child with my parents in Saint Louis and drove to the California Institute of Technology, in Pasadena. This part of California was beautiful in 1948. Pasadena was surrounded by orange groves and vineyards.

We put a down payment on a one-bedroom house and also charged a television set. Then I returned to Saint Louis to pick up our son. We returned by train to Pasadena. The first winter in California was extraordinarily cold. The soil in our yard was frozen down to three inches. This severe cold is rare in Southern California, and a lot of plants died. The citrus growers were firing up their smudge pots with oil to save the crops. On cold mornings the sky was black from the smudge fires. In those bygone days, there were fruit orchards everywhere.

Al was very busy in these early years of teaching. He was getting organized to teach classes, and he also wanted to see all the exciting geology of California—instantly.

One of the early major trips was to a place called Death Valley. I didn't know a thing about Death Valley except that I had seen the twenty-mule-team Borax ads on TV, and of course there was the series, "Death Valley Days," on TV and radio.

When the first geologic field trip was organized, men only, I asked if I could follow along in the red Studebaker. I would have to take our three-year-old son and our dog, but I would stay behind and not get in the way. No, I could not follow along. NO WOMEN ON FIELD TRIPS. Oh, that really irked me.

After they left, I fumed for a day and decided to go anyway. I was sure that I could find them somewhere. I was really crazy. There are thousands and thousands of square miles of desert. I did get a road map from a gasoline station and started north. There was really only the coastal road or the road through the San Joaquin Valley, or Highway 395, which went northeast through a lot of high desert. We could follow 395 and eventually turn east and find Death Valley. Yes, well, California is a very big state.

We did get to the main road into Death Valley and started down the long grade into the valley, from about five thousand feet or more, to a little below sea level. It was almost dark. I used the brakes so much hurrying downhill that soon I could smell them burning, that hot rubber smell. Then I used the gears to slow down. There was no traffic coming or going.

Finally, I saw a sign that read Stove Pipe Wells Motel and I went in there to ask for a room. They were filled, or so they said. It was late winter or early spring and rather chilly. Somehow I thought it should be hot here. Where should I go? What would they recommend? "Well, there is nothing but the Furnace Creek Inn, so try that," they said.

Death Valley was a dark hole in 1949, and they didn't have telephones to call around. Calls were radioed around the valley, and no one cared a damn about tourists. They thought I was some nut, clearly not a desert rat, who would know what to do in a desert.

It was a long, dark trip from Stove Pipe Wells to the Furnace Creek Inn. They did have a room, but it was very, very expensive, just about all the money I had, except for a little for gasoline the next day. I had to get out of this place after just one night. Maybe I could catch up with the men the next day. We didn't have a credit card for anything. Who did in those days? I don't know. The price of gasoline in the valley was forty cents a gallon. That was a rip-off in those days.

The dog was a problem, so I decided to leave him in the car. A man came out to carry the bags. We had a paper bag with pj's and diapers. Oh, we did have dog food along and a bowl for drinking water for the dog. I was struggling around in the car. The dome light would not turn off, and I started to take it apart with a screwdriver to remove the bulb so the battery wouldn't run down.

The man said "Lady, if you close the car door, the dome light will go out." Yes, well, I was very tired and dopy.

The inn was grand—really a very palatial place to stay—and breakfast was included in the price. I wish I could have enjoyed it more, but I was forever trying to think how to catch up with the men. I have always wanted to go back to the Furnace Creek Inn and stay for a week.

I knew the men had said they were going to Shoshone and out through Baker at the south end of the Death Valley Trough. So I started south on the road that is Number 178 now. It did not have a number then. I had a tankful of gasoline and two dollars left. We passed the lowest point in the continental U.S., minus 282 feet, and

Bad Water, and then the road just disappeared.

The east side of Death Valley has the largest, steepest alluvial fans in the world. There must have been a lot of floods out of the steep canyons or a tremendous snowmelt, because what little blacktop there was ended at the edge of new alluvial fans that covered the road. A few hearty pickup trucks must have been over this before me. I learned later that the men I was following didn't even take this route because they were warned not to take this road. There were boulders as big as the car where the road used to be, but somehow I threaded my way through these massive debris flows in that little red Studebaker.

Our son, who was standing to watch all this, finally became tired and lay down on my lap. Every time I hit another really bad place he would cry out, "What been that, Mommy?" He must have said that a hundred times. I kept patting him to calm him and myself. The dog got sick in the backseat. He was carsick from so many bumps and lurches. I didn't even have a bottle of water for us or the car. I saw one vehicle, a parked roadgrader, with no one around. Maybe this was Sunday? Maybe they had given up on the road? We finally reached Shoshone and Baker.

We used the two dollars for gasoline at Baker, and we chewed on Milkbone dog biscuits for dinner in the car. They are a little gritty with bone meal, I guess. We made it back to Pasadena late at night.

We had seen active, immense alluvial fans right up close and under us in one of the deepest valleys on earth.

The next day, I looked at the spare tire, because I worried about it all the way through the valley and beyond. It was not just low; it was flat.

Caltech

I had an enviable position. I worked for the U.S. Geological Survey, but I was allowed to work most of the time where my husband was teaching and our children lived.

The first institute was the California Institute of Technology in Pasadena. Caltech was relatively small when we arrived there in 1948. All of the buildings were beautiful, and the geology buildings were elegant. There were two buildings linked by a skywalk on the upper floor and gardens on the lower floor. The offices were large and the halls were wide and gleaming clean. The buildings were Spanish style, with ornately tiled drinking fountains and benches to rest on. The plantings were new to me—giant live oaks, palm trees, olive trees, and other semitropical plantings.

The sumptuous dining room was in the Athenaeum—a residence on campus for visiting scholars. Women were allowed to dine there. I went to one meeting at Berkeley, and the presence of a woman at lunch in the Faculty Club caused an uproar. Women had to eat in an annex, a shabby white building attached to the main dining room. Women had to parade through the tables of men to get to this porch-room where they were allowed to eat. That surprised me at Berkeley, because they had women professors. It didn't seem right that female professors had to hide in the outbuilding. Women were not considered "members of the club."

Caltech had a curious system pertaining to the bathrooms. One door read Men, and the next door read Faculty. Faculty members had a key to their private john, but they were all men. No women faculty and no female students were there at that time, at least not in the geological sciences.

There was only one john labeled Women in the whole building. The planners did think ahead, but only for the secretaries, which they needed very much. Or perhaps that facility was for visiting mothers or rich female trustees? I don't recall a female trustee either. I used to watch them arrive in their Cadillacs and Lincolns.

The dining room at the Athenaeum was decorated with hand-painted ceilings and brocade draperies. I used to sit in there and just stare around. It was lovely. I don't recall the food at all, but I think that lunch was a standard item. Waiters served a plate of food, and it was whatever was special for the day.

At first, I worked in Al's office, in the anteoffice. Then a large laboratory across the hall became available. It had sinks, gas and air lines, and a hood—everything I needed at the time. That laboratory had one drawback. Adjacent to the east window was a huge palm tree that reached to the second floor. When it was slightly windy, that palm tree swayed and swayed—back and forth. I tried not to look at the palm tree, but we could see it from every position in the room. We ordered a blind and kept it closed most of the time. Otherwise I would have been seasick and I wasn't at sea.

This lab had hardwood cabinets with doors that opened wide and reached to the ceiling. One section was full of fossils, small brachiopods, stored in little boxes in a sort of haphazard fashion. I needed the space, but I didn't know what to do with the fossils. From time to time, I went around asking, "Who owns the fossils?" No one knew. For two years, the brachiopods rested in the cabinet, and then one day, I thought, *Oh, the hell with them—throw them out.* That very afternoon, a young man, an ex-graduate student, came into the lab looking for the fossils. He had been gone for two years, all over the world, and now he had come back to finish his thesis.

I said, "You are lucky that I didn't throw them away." He was outraged. He thought he could leave his stuff around forever and it would still be there. Well, the fossils were there, and that is just about the way science used to be at Caltech. You could leave your specimens around almost anywhere. It was a far less stressful time than now. One could work on a problem for a century, and no one would interfere. Now, science, all sciences, are in a great frantic rush to "get finished." It was much more fun in the old days when you could work along for years on one project.

Most of the men in our building were young, too. Some of them visited with me. Many of them helped me with problems that came up. Graduate students were pleasant to me because many were my age. Later, at the Scripps Institution of Oceanography, I became the resident mother and grandmother.

In 1950 and later, the geology department was trying to add a group of geochemists. It was certainly the wave of the future—chemists who would attempt to solve geological problems. They had a lot of staff meetings at lunchtime that lasted for hours.

Then it started. Guys would come in after the staff meetings and Al wasn't back yet—he was still arguing. One of the men would say, "Al is crazy." Then he would rant and rave and I would keep working and agreeing with him. Mostly, each one wanted to let off steam about my husband. It was strange that they would come to Al's wife—me. At least I thought it was strange. I didn't tell Al what they said about him or the meeting, because a lot of times I wasn't listening. I had to keep thinking so as not to blow up the building or burn myself. Then Al would return to his office, usually the last one out of the meeting, and the visitors would stop, for at least that week.

My work was so slow that many evenings I went back to work for an extra few hours. A lot of graduate students worked at night. One worked most of the night. He had a huge furnace and vacuum extraction apparatus. It was a magnificent array of glass in the Hollywood concept of a science laboratory. He was extracting oxygen from rocks, minerals, and fossils for oxygen isotopic studies. He was very shy and he sat on the concrete floor next to his furnace. Sometimes he fell asleep, hunched down in the corner on the floor. We didn't talk at all, but we nodded to each other. I think he would have leaped up to help me if I had spilled acid all over myself, but I am not certain. He seemed rooted to his furnace. Several months later, he married the daughter of a faculty member in the physics department. I was astonished that he even talked to a woman.

Other students were busy planning to throw stink bombs or their damn water bombs. Or they switched the doors so the faculty members couldn't get into their bathroom. They placed pails of water over the doors. When the door opened, the unsuspecting person was soaked. The students spent a lot of time planning elaborate tricks. This was one of the first group of graduate students who had survived World War II. They were extra-crazy.

The geology department had an interesting head secretary, Miss Reno. She must have started with the department when it was formed at the very beginning. She knew everything and I had to tell her everything—even every uninteresting thing. For example, if I was at home and phoned to ask Al if we could go to a movie, I could not just ask her to have him phone me. I had to tell her about the movie, where it was, what time we had to get there, and on and on. I didn't mind in the least, but why did she want to know all that dull stuff? The staff was her family. She was brusque but kind to me. I called her Miss Reno. I did not call her by her first name, in fact, I didn't know her first name. I would have choked trying to use her first name.

The newly arrived geochemists were interesting. One member of the staff worked on lead isotopes. He determined the age of meteorites and thus the age of the earth at 4500 million years. He was well known all over the world. I did not understand exactly how he had proved the age of meteorites or on which meteorites(s). I asked him to explain to me. He sat down on my lab bench and I sat in a chair in front of him, and then he started to talk and talk and talk and I could not understand him at all. I must have looked dumb, because finally he asked, "Do you understand?" We could speak together on any subject but science. When he spoke about his scientific work, it was as if his mind was traveling on hundreds of diverse circuits. One thought led him to an unrelated fact, and then he would digress and I would get lost.

"No, I am sorry, but I don't understand." I hated to disappoint him, because he was trying earnestly to explain his research to me.

Then he would start over, or he would start in the middle or near the end. It was frustrating because I felt the concept was not that difficult. He should be able to explain to me. He didn't have a huge vocabulary, so I was not missing words that I did not understand. I was trying hard to understand him.

"I will bring you a paper. You can read about it," he

said. Good. He did bring the paper, published in *Geochemica Cosmochemica Acta*. Usually I can't remember who the publisher is, but I read it so many times that I couldn't forget. This was a reprint and it was not very long. I took the paper home and decided to read it in bed. I started to read. I read and reread the abstract, which was about one half-page long. I read it again and again, and nights later I was still trying to understand the abstract. I could not understand the writing either. I was just about to start crying.

Al was out of town, and when he came home I told him that I needed a lot of help. This genius, Paterson, had explained his theory to me and then given me a reprint, which I couldn't understand either. Besides, I liked Paterson very much.

"Oh, don't worry about that," Al said. "The guys who work with Paterson interpret his work for all of the rest of us. No one else can understand his explanations." What a shame to be that brilliant and not be able to explain. Paterson had many admirable traits, but the one that appealed to me was that he did all the worrying about their five children. When he and his wife were at a party, he would go home early to change diapers and check on their children. Perhaps he was worn out at age forty.

We parked at Caltech in a space printed Engel, and the next space was assigned to an astrophysicist. Sometimes we arrived at the same time. We said hello to him. That guy wanted to colonize the moon, our satellite. He told me that the U.S. would get to the moon and that we would make oxygen from limestone (calcium carbonate) on the moon.

"But no one thinks there is limestone on the moon."

He brushed that aside and went on to water. "We will get water from serpentine [hydrated Mg-silicate]."

"But why would the moon contain serpentine? The moon never had water with which to form the mineral serpentine." (I added the brackets, because I don't think the astrophysicist knew the composition of the rocks and minerals he mentioned.) I was always in a daze after we had one of our brief encounters. What was I missing? What was he missing?

He stopped talking to me. He just nodded if we arrived in the parking lot at the same time. But he did publish his wild ideas; I read about them later.

We also had a lot of brilliant guys who could explain anything. I am not picking on the whole Caltech group. A few of the early geochemists came to me with thin sections of rocks they wanted to work on. One came in with a thin section that he said was full of zircons. He wanted to extract zircons from the rock and date the rock. I don't know why he was looking at zircons, because he was a potassium/argon age man at that time. He would have to get the age of the rock from the whole rock or the potassium-feldspar minerals.

"Let's look at the zircons." I uncovered our petrographic microscope and clamped the thin section to the stage. The rock was a granitic rock with many crystals of apatite—no zircons, not even one or two tiny crystals. Well, perhaps if I had gone to a higher power, I could have found a few minute zircons. As one chemist told me never put down zero, use "trace" instead. Then if the next scientist finds something, you can repeat, "I said *trace*."

Now this young professor with the granitic slide full of apatite, not zircon, was brilliant and proud, and he might just blow up if he became angry. So I had to use my dumb-female technique, which I hate to do.

"I don't think these dull gray crystals are zircon—perhaps they are apatite—but let's look them up in *Optical Properties of Minerals*. Would you please look up apatite in the index and find the page for me?" That worked. The book said that apatite was clear to pale gray in plain light, not pleochroic, poorly formed crystals, and in polarized light still dull gray, and on and on. He looked into the microscope and said, "This is apatite."

He didn't mention zircon, nor did I. Did he ever come back with another thin section for me to look at? I can't remember, but I think not. However, I still like him.

There was a graduate student, Lee Silver, a very bright guy. He was a graduate student for so long that he finally turned into a faculty member. He is still at Caltech. I went to a few seminars with him. We sat together a lot. Then one day it was his turn to give a seminar. The poor lad was so nervous. His mouth was dry, his hands shook, and he perspired so much under his arms that he soaked his shirt. I suffered along with him. It is a wonder to me that he managed to survive without a stroke or heart attack. He was nervous, but tough. Now he gives talks everywhere and likes to talk to big groups. He can't be shaking still(?).

Owl Creeks

Al took a group of students from Caltech to geology camp in the Owl Creek Mountains of Wyoming. He knew the mountains well, since he had worked in them for years while he was a graduate student in the late 1930s.

In those early days, Al saw elk, deer, antelope, and bears; he even heard about a grizzly bear but didn't see it. He worked on horseback so he could cover about 1,200 square miles of the Owl Creek Mountains. A sheepherder came screaming into Al's camp one day yelling that a grizzly bear had torn up his camp. From then on, Al slept with a sawed-off shotgun next to his bedroll. He hung most of his food in the limbs of trees so that bears would not feast on food while he was away from camp. At night, he hobbled his horse and both of them stayed in a clearing. Al hoped his horse would give him warning if anything came near camp. Horses are afraid of bears, and they become restive and noisy if a bear is near. One of his horses stood still all night, staring into the forest. That scared Al, too.

Of course, I would have given up on the day the sheepherder saw a grizzly. They are big animals, and they travel long distances to forage for food. But Al made the mountains sound romantic. And he learned they were romantic mountains, because occasionally he was able to camp near a homestead. The man of the house was Irish, and the lady of the house a Shoshone. They had five beautiful daughters.

The core of the mountains is about 3,000 million years old. Within this core are the remnants of an ancient ocean floor and island arc partially broken and enveloped by granitic rocks. This rock mass was cut by hundreds of parallel dikes of gabbro, the coarse-grained equivalent of basalt. All of this ancient Earth's crust had undergone several stages of mountain building and erosion, with only the central and root parts of the ancient complex still visible. Younger oceans had covered the roots of the mountains about 550 million years ago and laid down a sequence of fascinating sedimentary rocks from 550 to 160 million years old. Then the whole complex was again folded and faulted into mountains between 160 and 60 million years ago. The Owl Creek Mountains are part of the central Rocky Mountains.

Our sons and I watched the group of students and two faculty members get ready to go to Wyoming. They had to drag everything along, including a generator, a refrigerator, tents, cots, bedrolls, cooking utensils, and antivenom kits for rattlesnake bites—just in case.

I couldn't visualize where they planned to camp, but Al said they would camp on Cottonwood Creek. Every state in the West has several Cottonwood Creeks.

Al told me that they would get mail at the post office in Thermopolis, Wyoming. We could write to him in Wyoming.

He said, "They will know in Thermopolis where we are. Also, you can ask for directions to the Todd Ranch. Mrs. Todd will cook for us, and she will tell you where we are camped."

Al didn't plan for us to get to Wyoming or find the camp. However, the children and I planned to get there.

I don't know how many times we have crossed the desert from Pasadena, California to Salt Lake City and beyond by car. It was far too many times, but we did have a new mountain range to explore in Wyoming if we made the trip. Today we have an air-conditioned car, but in those days only Cadillacs had air-conditioning. I used to curse at the Cadillac owners who sailed by with windows rolled up and not a hair out of place. Our car always turned into a garbage heap after the first day.

We stayed at a motel south of Salt Lake City on the second night. I saw a gardener with some chickens clucking around at his feet while he worked in a garden next to the motel. That is when I took the heavy chain from under the seat and attached the dog to the bumper. He was a bird hunting dog, a setter, and was looking at the chickens when we were unpacking the car. When the boys and I got the last bag into the motel and were coming out to lock the car, that evil dog gave a mighty pull, broke the chain, and headed for the chickens. *We will be in jail here,* I thought. I yelled "NO," and the dog stopped. Bad dog—good dog.

The next day, we drove to Wyoming and came in on the southwest side of the Owl Creek Mountains. The southern sun-baked side of the Owl Creek Mountains was ugly, hot, desolate, steep, and almost devoid of vegetation. It was July or August. Most of Wyoming is high desert, with a few lovely places in the high mountains.

We went north through the majestic Wind River Canyon to the post office at Thermopolis, Wyoming, and asked for mail. Maybe we would have a note in General Delivery. There was not even a postcard for us.

"Do you know where the Caltech geology group is camped?" I asked the postmaster.

"No, but some of them come in here for mail now and then."

"Where is the Todd ranch, please?"

"Out on the Owl Creek road about twelve miles." No one planned for us to get to the geology camp, not the postmaster and not Albert.

We found the Todd ranch, a miserable run-down homestead with a few skinny cows. The sun was low and glared off the oiled road. One of the boys said, "Why don't you get out of the car and call for Dad? He may be just over the next hill."

I got out on the road and yelled, "Albert!" a few times and heard my echo off the hot sedimentary rocks of the hills. *What am I doing out here in the middle of nowhere yelling, "Albert?" That—that, crazy Albert.* I thought of a lot of adjectives that would apply to him and to me, too, for following crazy Albert.

We went back to Thermopolis and rented a cabin. In

the West, where it is hot and dry all summer, tourists fall into bed early and get up early, too early. At about 4:30 A.M. they start leaving motels and they yell a lot or they talk loudly. "Joe do you have the water bottle?" "Is Minnie in the car?" "I'm hungry." Then they slam the doors, start the motors, pump the accelerators, and leave.

We got up, too, ate breakfast, and hurried back to the Todd ranch. We caught Mrs. Todd just as she was leaving the ranch to go back to the geology camp. She said, "It's up there in the mountains."

Mrs. Todd didn't plan for us to find the geology camp either. She was most unfriendly.

She was driving a truck, and we had an old Plymouth station wagon. "May we follow you?"

"Can't stop ya." She could have told me and she should have told me that no ordinary car could get way up there in those rugged mountains, but she didn't. The only road was the one Al made to get into camp, and that was full of boulders, holes, outcrops of rock and it was high up and hot. The Plymouth finally stalled and we were only halfway up. Mrs. Todd did take us the rest of the way in her truck. She probably would have left us, but she was worried about her job and also being charged with involuntary manslaughter if we died in the mountains because we couldn't get to the camp.

Albert always picks a beautiful campsite. We were on the north face of the mountains in a high mountain meadow with scattered trees and beautiful wild flowers everywhere. The middle fork of Cottonwood Creek crossed through the camp area, and they had dug a pond so they could get a lot of captured trout in one pool. Then they could fish in peace. The creek was quite small—you could jump across it—and it was full of fat trout. The water was so low that the trout had to live under the grassy banks. When they moved about, they skittered across the rocky bottom of the stream with their dorsal fins out of the water. Any trout fisherman would have gone crazy to see so many plump, hungry fish.

We assured ourselves that we had to eat the trout to save them from drying up.

This was all Indian reservation at the time, Arapaho and Shoshone. The Indians ran some cattle in the mountains. Some of the cattle were alive, but many were dead and not too long ago. Bloated bodies were lying all over the place. I don't think the Indians gave them shots for all the cattle diseases. On the other hand, perhaps shots were not available then. We saw elk, deer, and antelope in groups of five to fifty roaming around near the cattle and the salt blocks. The Indians did put out salt for the cattle.

Al pitched a tent for us, a dark-green heavy, large tent. Most days the tent was like an oven—hot. But at night the temperature plummeted and it was very cold. We were at an elevation of 6,000 feet. We had a few violent hailstorms with ice balls the size of golf balls. Our younger son was sleeping in a down-filled mummy bag, and most nights he managed to get upside down in the bag and started to scream for help. That is why geologists don't want their families along. They are too much trouble.

In the daytime, the boys and I picked flowers or caught grasshoppers for the hungry trout. We would each get a bottle of grasshoppers and throw them into the pond. The water boiled as the trout gulped the grasshoppers. I don't know how all these trips affected our sons. One became a biologist and he is always roaming around the way we did. It was hard for him to find a home. The other turned into an artist, but he always takes vacations in wildlife sanctuaries. He called recently from Texas to tell us that he saw thousands of snow geese and was able to walk among them. He said they made a lot of noise. Being out of doors in so many different places caused them to catch onto the biological end, but they hated geologists.

I don't understand how men survive when they are living together.

It seems that since the days in the caves, women have tried to tidy up a bit. The mess tent was a mess. The dishes were not clean. I started putting a bit of ammonia in the dish-washing water—over Mrs. Todd's dead body. She started to loosen up a bit when I started helping her wash and dry the dishes. I tried to kill her with kindness.

One morning after breakfast, after all the geologists were gone into the field, I took the antivenom kits out of the refrigerator and started to read how to use the stuff in case of rattlesnake bites. The first warning is that children or small people might need more antivenom than adults, because their bodies contain less fluids. Then you have to mix the antivenom material with distilled water on the spot. Would creek water do? I guess we could use it because it was melted snow water. Before all of that, you must test the person for a reaction to horse serum. A lot of people are allergic to horse serum. The directions and warnings became more and more complicated. I put the kit back into the refrigerator. I would not have used the stuff on anyone unless they were gasping for the last breath. Then it probably would be too late.

Al demanded a lot from the students, and some of them became surly. They didn't want to live so far from everything and crawl over the mountains all day long. City kids. Al was always going to send one or two home on the bus. Another student was cold all the time. He wore an aviator's suit from World War II. He had a lot of wires attached to batteries in order to keep warm. But the batteries failed and then he put long johns under the lined suit. Another came down with a severe case of mononucleosis and spent the summer in the hospital at Thermopolis.

An earnest student was reading the Book of Mormon to our children in the evenings. They liked to listen to him, but it didn't take.

The Indians have closed the Owl Creek Mountains to white men. I would have kept the mountains to myself if I owned them. Perhaps some geologists or Fish and Game people can get permission to go in and stay a while. All the rest of us have to stay out. Here was one place where the Indians retained some magnificent country and wildlife. I hope they are taking care of it.

Punch Bowl

When I was thirty-three, I went to UCLA to do graduate work and earn an advanced degree. Years before, I had lost my thesis and most of my notes from graduate school. I left all of it, all that hard work, in the backseat of a taxi in Washington, D.C.

My advisor and mentor at UCLA said that first I would have to take a lot of courses in mathematics. I did that and enjoyed it very much. But if you work all day in a lab, then come home and prepare dinner and get the children to bed, you are in bad shape to tackle big problems in calculus at night on the kitchen table. I often thought that the math problems were so complicated and long that I really needed all night to get ready for the next math class at eight o'clock in the morning. My husband helped me a lot.

Then I complicated my life even further by enrolling in a class in the Russian language. Russian lessons could take all day and part of the night, but Al and I thought that we should know what the Russians were writing about in the earth sciences. No one was translating Russian journals the way they are now. We became good enough in the Russian language to read titles, abstracts, and of course tables containing chemical data that we wanted to relate to our work.

In those days, all incoming students at UCLA had to have a physical examination. I wonder if they are still doing that. We had to stand in a hallway in the basement of the medical building wrapped in a sheet. Hundreds of women wrapped in sheets! Even the graduate students were standing around in sheets. I thought this was just for kids out of high school. Later, I realized that the medical school probably had grants from the NIH to study human females and there we were—all ages, sizes, colors, and shapes.

At last, classes started in geology.

One of the first courses I took was optical mineralogy. I thought this would be easy for me, since I knew all there was to know about minerals already. Not so. This professor dragged out minerals I had never seen and will never see again. What was very bad about the class was that we had absolutely nothing on the common minerals, which number less than one hundred varieties. I didn't do as well as I thought I would. I was irked most of the time about struggling with these exotic minerals that the professor bought from Wards Scientific.

The professor purchased oriented mineral sections, cut and glued to a glass slide with a specific axis of the crystal vertical, or lying horizontal to the field of view, or neither. It is much easier to identify a mineral if it is presented in a rock matrix. That way you can identify the rock in which it crystalized. I spent a week on a crystal of epidote, a secondary mineral that usually occurs in a granitic rock. Epidote is a "garbage can" mineral, a silicate with various amounts of water in the crystal lattice. Of course, I had seen it before, but not so large a slice. This mineral covered the whole field of view. It was pale yellowish-green, a good clue, or I would still be hanging over it trying to identify it.

Here I could not use the indices of refraction with immersion oils. I had to use the petrographic microscope to get optical figures. I was swearing to myself, but learning a bit. Many times when I looked at the interference figures they were opposite of what the lab instructor said. Was I color-blind? Was he? Perhaps both. The colors using a quartz wedge didn't look correct to me either. Our lab instructor stuttered, so I didn't want to argue with him or otherwise upset him.

My last mineral was apatite, a phosphate mineral, dull gray with no clue at all under the microscope—just a big mass of gray. I had seen that mineral, too, in metamorphic and igneous rocks. But no one wants to see a slide full of it. I didn't learn much in optical mineralogy. Then the professor asked me if I would like to make quantitative chemical analyses of a suite of rocks from the Sierra Nevada for him. He had thin sections for me of every rock. I learned a lot from doing the chemical analyses of igneous rocks of the Sierra Nevada, and the professor published a paper on the chemistry of the Sierra rocks.

We had a professor who came from the U.S. Geological Survey. He was a guest lecturer for one year. I knew his work. He put together one of the first geological maps of the United States, but he couldn't teach at all. He wrote elegant, clear papers on various subjects, but he couldn't speak. He seemed extremely bashful. He was not going to lecture at all. We were going to present papers for him. I am a bashful speaker, also, and I did understand, but he should not have been teaching at UCLA. He put a lot of little folded papers in a beaker, and we each drew three subjects on which to present a seminar. I had granitization, oolites (more on that later), and oil deposits in stratigraphic traps.

I would start with granitization because I felt I knew most about that subject. Al and I had worked in metamorphic terrains where we thought many rock units were granitized. Granitizing fluids are inferred to seep into the country rock from underlying magmas. The fluids are Si-Al-K-rich and, replace original rocks and change the compostion to a more granitic type. The process is much more complicated, but I liked the hypothesis. We thought we saw many examples of granitized rocks in the northwest Adirondack Mountains.

I learned all of my worst geologic habits from Al. I accepted many (all) of his views and carried them into my classes.

The seminar table was U-shaped, with chairs facing toward a blackboard. I knew that I would be a nervous wreck standing in front of the other students trying to speak and that the notes in my hand would tremble because my whole arm was shaking. So I devised a scheme. I would write some information on the blackboard and then ease backward until I could sit on the edge of the table. Somehow, being partly seated helped to control my stage fright, and while sitting I could hold my shaking arm with the other hand and steady my whole body.

When I drove to UCLA in the afternoon for these seminars, I thought of having a cocktail on the way—to steady my nerves and make me a bold, convincing speaker. I didn't do that either for fear of just getting sick. Right off, I found that Dr. King *did not believe in granitization.* He didn't like me at all after the first seminar.

Oolites are very small concretions that form in sediments. They are almost microscopic in size, but if you have good eyesight you can see them with the unaided eye or better with a hand lens. The scientist who wrote most about oolites discovered that some were deformed from spheres into ellipsoids by rock deformation. But who cares? I did better on that seminar because I wasn't interested in oolites and had no strong opinions.

On statigraphic traps and oil deposits I did best of all. I had good illustrations and I could understand three-dimensional structures, while some of the students could understand only two-dimensional structures.

Al told me that some students in his field geology classes could not project a folded rock unit into the earth. They could not think in three dimensions.

Then we closed the semester with a field trip to the Punch Bowl on the northeast side of the San Gabriel Mountains. I was excited about this because, although I had driven by these tilted rocks on the Cajon Pass Road, I had not seen the structures up close. We didn't have university transporation for the field course. Dr. King asked us to bring personal automobiles, I was to pick up two students from the east end of the San Gabriel Valley. The rest of the group would start from the UCLA campus.

We had a new dark red Buick that we were making

payments on, and I loved that car. I felt like an important person when I drove it. Students who didn't have transportation were supposed to ride in one of the cars and pay for the gasoline. Fine.

"Dr. King, will an ordinary auto be able to make this trip, or do we need a truck?" Remember, I asked him.

I had two guys in my car and they were paying for the gasoline and the road was beautiful right to the entrance sign, which said Devil's Punch Bowl. We walked for part of the day and saw the structures, which were all tilted, fractured, and folded along the trace of the San Andreas Fault Zone. Then we got into the cars again and started up a rock road. It was a road for a four-wheel-drive vehicle like those used by water and power personnel when they were driving through dry riverbeds. We were in a riverbed.

I was just sick about what I had to drive over and scrap over. The car got hung up and we had to shovel rocks out of the "road" to get the car through.

Even the devil couldn't drive over this road to his Punch Bowl. Then I was younger and quiet. Now I would kill a geologist who made me drive my new car over that same road.

On the Road Again

Al and I were working on the Leadville limestone in Colorado, and we found we couldn't afford to live in motels and eat in restaurants. We had our two boys along, and they were a lot of extra expense. So what to do?

I decided to drive back to Pasadena with the boys and just stay home. When we arrived back home, the summer weather was hot and smoggy. After a week, I thought, *why not rent a little house trailer and pull that back to Colorado?* We could eat and sleep in the trailer, and we could spill over into a tent if necessary. With a trailer we could also move around to different field locations with all of the maps, notes, clothes, food, and stuff with us. We had a lot of mountain showers in Colorado, and with a trailer, we could keep our notes and maps dry. It seemed like a great idea.

So I went to a trailer place and started asking about costs involved in renting a trailer.

The rental man said, "What are you gonna pull it with?" He was nervous about renting his equipment to a woman.

"Well, this Plymouth station wagon." It was a little car with a small engine, and the shift was on the wheel.

"You can't make it," the guy said.

"I'll try. Give me the smallest trailer you have."

It was fifteen feet long, and they said that it would sleep six, but I don't know where. The trailer had one narrow double bed, a canvas hammock to sling overhead, and if you put the table outside, made the seats into a bunk, and put all the clothes on the floor, you could get two adults and two children in it.

So we rigged up the back of the car with brake lights for the trailer and clamped a trailer ball on the rear bumper of the car. In addition, state law required a safety chain to be attached to the bumper and trailer in case the trailer came loose. I had nightmares about the trailer coming loose, because then the trailer would be hanging onto the car by a chain, flopping about and maybe pulling the car off the road. Always, I could worry ahead.

My mother was concerned about us. She was an angel. She couldn't drive, but she was willing to navigate for me. She offered to ride along, and I was glad to have her for the moral support. Our sons loved her, too.

Then I went to get the trailer. We were going to fill it with everything we needed to get back to Colorado. We planned to leave at three the next morning. Right off, I realized that I could not back up the car with the trailer attached. I had to back the trailer into our driveway, and I was lucky this one time—the driveway sloped down from the road so the trailer rolled backward into the driveway, all crooked, and the trailer dragged the car into the driveway, too.

My mother stood watching. "Perhaps you should not try to back up again," she said. Mother always managed to couch her fears in a polite negative fashion. We had to go straight ahead or drive in big circles. No more trying to back up when the trailer was hitched on.

Mother and I put the rear seat down and made beds for the boys. We would drag them out of bed, put them in the car with the dog, and head for Colorado. We had to get out of the Los Angeles basin and over Cajon Pass (four thousand feet) before the day became very hot. We didn't have trailer brakes either.

In 1953, Cajon Pass was two lanes wide. Now the road is eight lanes wide. We did just fine until we got halfway up the pass. The sun was just coming up, and the road was cool. There was a big truck ahead, and we were grinding away. My mother looked around the truck and said, "Dear, you can pass the truck now." She didn't know that our accelerator was on the floor and we were going about twenty-five miles per hour—top speed. We were lucky to be going forward at all. When I explained all that, she said, "Oh." We didn't talk much. She may have been praying.

We did fairly well for most of the rest of the day, but we studied each gasoline station to be certain we were on the right side for the gas tank and that we could get back on the highway without backing up. We made it okay up the huge grade out of Baker, California. That used to be a car and truck killer, perhaps it still is. However, we did get into a lot of trouble on the long grade onto what is called the Colorado Plateau, northeast of Las Vegas.

From Saint George, Utah, to Cedar City is a huge, long grade, and it was late afternoon and very hot. We had to stop about every two hundred feet in elevation and let the car cool off, but we could all sit in the trailer and drink pop. Our younger son built little teepees of sticks along the side of the road. He built them so well that we saw them there for years. The last one fell over or rotted or blew away about five years later.

We rented a motel in Cedar City, one with a big turnaround area. My mother and the boys slept inside. I took a shower and went to sleep in the trailer. I remember hearing the warm breeze in the trees, a pleasant rustling sound, and then nothing for twelve hours. I have never been so tired.

I think that we made it back to our appointed rendezvous in Glenwood Springs, Colorado, in two and a half days. We considered that great time for a long, slow trip.

When we saw Al, he said, "What took you so long?"

Who says you should not kill your husband? How about sticking him with the big butcher knife in the trailer?

The Russians Are Coming

When we learned that the first Russian geologist was coming to visit us at the California Institute of Technology, I was very excited. He was D. S. Korzhinsky, a distinguished member of the Soviet Academy of Sciences. Al and I read some of his work, slowly and laboriously, with help from a Russian translator. We can be thankful that the Russians have the same numbers and symbols for elements.

Korzhinsky was very interested in metamorphic rocks—rocks altered by heat and pressure at depth in the earth and then eroded and exposed at the surface during mountain building.

He came to Pasadena, California, and then we took him to a metamorphic rock complex near Palm Springs, California. There were four of us in a GMC carryall. I drove, because I could watch Korzhinsky in the backseat in the rearview mirror. I wondered if he was a spy. I was stupid. We headed east on a highway and passed a steel mill. Korzhinsky didn't look at that—he just kept talking and rarely looked out the windows. This surprised me, because I would have been curious about a Russian landscape. His English was good. He was polite, low-key, and charming—a very pleasant person. This was going to be fun.

This Russian scientist had kept his eminent position through the last days of Czar Nicholas, through Stalin, to Khrushchev.

Our other passenger was a famous geologist from Cambridge, England, Prof. Cecil Tilley. Tilley and Korzhinsky were about the same age, and for some reason,

I still don't know why, Tilley did not like the Russian. Tilley made a lot of sarcastic remarks. I hoped that Korzhinsky didn't understand most of them, but perhaps he did. It must have been some sort of super-professional jealousy. Al and I tried to treat these men exactly alike.

In the early 1950s, Palm Springs was a small town with a lot of desert around it. We looked at all the rock units. Korzhinsky collected quite a few samples. There was nothing commercial here, just good examples of metamorphic geology.

Then we went to the area of Palm Canyon. This southern portion of Palm Springs and every other section of land in the area was owned by the Agua Caliente Indians. We had to pay to get in to view the palm groves and the little streams that trickled down from Mount San Jacinto above. Of course, we were on a gigantic fault zone, which was part of the San Andreas Fault system. Korzhinsky was fascinated by that. It reminded him of southern Soviet territory, where huge active faults, with earthquakes, were similar in structure.

The palm groves consist of *Washingtonia filifera* palms, which are native to this part of California and northern Mexico. They are supposed to have existed in oases for over a thousand years, but we found fossil palm wood that was much older.

The Spanish named the area Agua Caliente for the warm springs nearby.

What Korzhinsky was most surprised about was that white people were employed to run the Palm Canyon Park and the concessions for the Indians.

He asked, "White people work for Indians?" Yes, yes. I guess he thought that whites had stolen all Indian land. That we did do most everywhere in the United States, but this barren desert was not considered important at the time. The Aqua Caliente Indians were a small group, less than one hundred people, owning much worthless desert. Now they are rich Indians.

For a late lunch, we went to an outdoor café in old Palm Springs. It was very pleasant. The shop next door was having a fashion show, with models strolling about in elegant clothes.

I said, "Oh, look, you can see a fashion show."

Korzhinsky blushed, turned away, and said, "My wife not like for me to look."

I thought that he meant that he shouldn't look at the models in swimsuits and play clothes. I was sort of uncomfortable, too, because the atmosphere was one of capitalistic luxury at its worst. Much later it dawned on me that Korzhinsky thought these models were prostitutes. After all, where would he see a fashion show in the Soviet Union in those days? Now, yes, but then, no.

The whole Palm Springs area was a shock to him and to me, too, come to think of it. Indians controlling the fate of the richest desert playground on earth, with white people working for the Indians—yes, it was truly a puzzle.

Now Palm Springs is a fair-sized city with less desert around it. People moved farther and farther out and covered the sand with homes. Then the late arrivals moved up into the boulders of the alluvial fans and finally into the bedrock. Many of our favorite exposures of metamorphic rocks are now covered with streets, houses, condos, and golf courses.

There were lots of other Russians who came to Scripps—geologists, oceanographers, biologists, and geochemists—but the pair I enjoyed the most was a man/woman team. I don't think they were teamed up to work together before this trip, but they came to La Jolla, California, to the Scripps Institution of Oceanography to join an expedition at sea. They were going to the South Pacific on a United States research vessel.

I could tell Elena had packed in a hurry. She said she had one day's notice. She opened her suitcase to ask about her clothes, and everything was in a big jumble, as if she had snatched it from drawers and crammed the lid shut. Everything popped out and some of the items were eyepoppers. She held up a swimsuit. It looked like fishing net with no lining whatever.

Elena asked, "This suitable on boat?" Now that I think about it, why was I so stuffy? I didn't know what to say without offending her, so I just stared at the suit.

She said, "Suit not right." Well, yes, no, or maybe. Where did she plan to wear it? We got off the swimsuit topic. She really didn't have a thing to wear that would last for thirty days at sea.

The man Gleb carried all the money. I know because he asked me to take him to a bank in La Jolla, any bank. Elena and I waited in the car. I sat in front and she was in the backseat. La Jolla is a wealthy town with well-dressed people shopping around and very expensive cars parked in the streets.

We were quiet for a while. Then Elena asked, "How many autos you have?"

We had three but I said, "Two."

"Oh," she said, "I look to have one auto soon." She was a capitalist. She wanted to buy everything.

Gleb came out of the Bank of America with a fistful of twenty-dollar bills, with some larger bills rolled in the middle. It took him quite a while to get some wedged into his billfold and others crammed into his pants pocket. I was dying to ask, "What are you going to do with all that money?" but I didn't.

We went to shop at the stores in Fashion Valley in

San Diego. They bought tennis shoes to wear on the ship. He bought good ones for himself, but a cheaper pair for her. They bought jeans and shirts. I noted that he always had two to one of hers. It wasn't fair, because as I learned later, she had a much better brain. She just couldn't get him to spend any money on her.

Then, since there was some time left, I took them to the desert east of San Diego. Elena claimed not to have seen a cactus. She and Gleb discussed that in Russian. I could follow just a bit of their conversations, but I did have a big question to ask, so I did. Would they please explain to me about the aspects of Russian verbs? I didn't ask the question properly, because they argued with each other in Russian for half an hour, some of it quite heated, but I didn't get an answer.

It took a visit from Academician A. P. Vinogradov, a tiny little old man who headed nine institutes in Moscow, to help me with aspects. Vinogradov had a good-looking female translator with him. He did not want to talk about geology or geochemistry. All he wanted to do was pick oranges and drink orange juice. Fortunately, we lived in an orange grove. Vinogradov said that he worked too much. His wife was dead and one of his two sons had been killed fighting Germans at the Battle of Leningrad. His remaining son worked as a surgeon and was very busy.

I was to write to Vinogradov about something. So I said, "Ya peeshoo vam [I write to you]."

"Nyet," he said, "Ya, napeeshoo vam." The former means that I will write and write and keep writing, the latter means that I will write once or twice and not again. Right then I understood what we call the aspects. But the more I learn, the less I know.

One thing is clear—the younger Russian scientists

did not understand the grammar of their language. They learned to speak correctly by examples in everyday use at school. The old man tried to teach me. All were grateful that I tried to speak Russian at all.

We had another visitor from the Soviet Union, Leonid Dimitriev, a young man who was working on rocks of the ocean floor, as we were. After a day at the laboratory, he came to our home and fell to the floor and cuddled our dog.

Dimitriev said, "I do not remember, but my mother said we had to eat our dog during World War II."

Chemistry

Al and I worked a long time with maps, reports, and thin sections of rocks from the northwest Adirondacks Mountains. New York, but we needed much more data. Particularly we needed chemical analyses of the whole rocks and of the minerals we had separated from the rocks. For example, we noticed that mica (biotite) changed color from greenish-brown to reddish-brown as the rocks were subjected to more heat and pressure at greater depths in the earth. These were all metamorphic rocks. The main rock unit that we hoped to analyze in detail was a dirty sandstone converted by heat and pressure into what is called a gneiss (pronounced "nice").

At that time, the U.S. Geological Survey in Denver had a fine laboratory for chemical analyses of rocks and minerals, but we had to get in line and wait for so long that sometimes we would forget the problem before we received data for a solution.

Fortunately, among the chemists in Prof. Harrison Brown's group at Caltech was one Bill Blake. He had trained at the Denver lab and then moved to Pasadena. Blake actually hoped to leave and become a dentist, but for now, and fortunately for me, he was in my clutches, or vice versa.

Blake was always immaculate, with a pressed white lab coat (no acid or other holes), and he agreed to let me work with him. He made lots of rules. If I spilled acid or otherwise messed up his place, I would be out. And all of the beakers with stirring rods in them had to face left, lined up in a neat row on the lab bench. That really stuck in my brain. Sometimes, thirty years later, when I look at a Coke can, I am tempted to turn it so the hole is to the left. Brainwashing works.

Blake agreed to let me observe and I could learn how to analyze a rock for the more abundant elements: silicon, aluminum, iron, calcium, magnesium, sodium, potassium, titanium, phosphorus, and water. I have omitted a few elements, and, of course, water is not an element.

At the same time, I was taking advanced courses in geology at UCLA under Professor Tunnell, a mineralogist. Tunnell was my advisor. I said, "I don't know what I am doing and why these various chemical processes are working at all."

"Never mind that," said Tunnell. "Just learn how to do it, and you can worry about what is happening later." It was excellent advice. Don't worry about understanding it all now, just learn Blake's methods.

I did finish partial analyses of samples G-1 and W-1. These were standard rock samples sent around the world to check the accuracy of other labs. Of course, I didn't know that at the time. But the amounts of these elements that I obtained on these rocks were good enough to earn me a white lab coat, plus some platinum crucibles. Big stuff.

Blake told me that if I got a hole in the coat or scratched the crucibles, I was finished in his laboratory. Okay, so I was very careful.

Then instead of starting on something like a simple granitic rock, or any rock, I tried to do a sample of garnet, a mineral, that we had laboriously separated from a metamorphic rock.

I used .5 grams of the garnet and 5 grams of sodium carbonate to fuse the garnet in a 30 milliliter platinum crucible. Right off, that sample with high iron content fused into the platinum crucible. It looked like glassy fudge, and only part of the fusion came out of the crucible. Blake was astounded, but he had never tried to analyze a garnet. Now we were learning together.

Blake made a lot of calls to Denver while I sat most of the day sanding the platinum crucible. Fortunately, the damage to the crucible was only skin deep, and I managed to get it back to fine shiny shape. I almost lost the fingerprints on two fingers polishing away on the crucible with wet quartz sand. I also lost about one-half a gram of platinum from the crucible.

Perhaps Blake's work was uninteresting or there wasn't enough of it, because from then on he had to see everything I did, and I became more fussy than he. He would see me throw out a fusion and start over.

"That fusion was good enough. You should have gone on with it," Blake said.

"No, it isn't good enough for me," I said. We changed places. I became the bitch in the laboratory, and he had acid holes in his coat.

We finally made a good fusion of garnet by adding 0.5 grams of sodium nitrite. Through the weeks and months that we were together we tried all sorts of strange rocks and minerals. We did have to call Mr. Lee Peck at the Denver lab for a lot of advice, and generally he was gracious and helpful. But Peck, who was one of the world's best rock and mineral analysts, was fussy, too, and not always cheerful. He would say, "I don't know what you are trying to do out there, but it can't be right." Or "You cause more trouble than the whole staff here."

Peck had a curious philosophy. He did have some excellent chemists in his unit, but he treated each sample as an unknown. That is, he didn't tell the staff what to expect on any given sample. He just handed them a vial of ground-up powder. I visited one time, and while on a coffee break, when Peck was out of the room, I said to the chemists, "You have a good library here. If you have a mineral or rock which is labeled, go look up the general composition in mineralogy or petrology textbooks. Don't work in the dark." Or they could go back to the original paperwork that had to be submitted with the request for chemical work. The geologists who sent in the samples had to name the rock or mineral.

Peck would not have liked that, but half the group went to the other building, which housed the library, and checked out books on rocks and minerals. They smiled a lot after they looked in the books. This sort of chemical work is difficult and slow, so why fly blind?

I was in Denver to learn their methods for determining fluorine and chlorine. My God, it was difficult and time-consuming. The fluorine method involved a titration with a curious lavender-green end point. Peck was stirring the solution, and he said, "Vicki, tell me when I am getting near the correct color." I looked at her, apparently with a question in my eyes, and she nodded yes. Peck was color-blind. After I studied their analytical procedures for several days, I decided I didn't care about fluorine or chlorine. I would just stay away from samples that required all this extra work.

The very best chemist in the Denver laboratory was Vicki Smith, a black woman. She helped me a great deal. She spent part of her time traveling for the U.S. Geological Survey in a motor home in order to recruit women and minorities. They carried displays of maps, air photos, and some lab equipment, and Vicki was in charge of making the sales pitch to young students everywhere in the West. Several years later, the rock and mineral analyses labs in Denver burned in a spectacular fire. I don't know if they were rebuilt.

Most of the analytical methods in our lab and in the Denver labs were gravimetric and photometric. It was slow work. Various groups around the country were trying to do analyses more rapidly. The U.S. Geological Survey laboratory in Washington, D.C., developed the so-called Rapid Method. I tried some of their methods, but they were not much faster.

Then X-ray fluorescence came along, and it is fairly good. Everything depends on equipment and the chemist doing the work. Equipment that is used by many operators usually fails in less than a year. Some strong man/woman must control the whole lab and equipment, or students will get in a hurry and mess up everything. Faculty members who are hurrying mess up, too.

Many institutes now use a microprobe for the composition of individual minerals. This method is usually much more expensive, due to the equipment needed, but that is okay if you have the money. All of the more recent methods require many "standard" rocks and minerals of known composition so one could produce a working curve.

One of the most expensive methods for chemical analyses is neutron activation. You must have your own atomic pile. We were close to General Atomic in La Jolla, and some of the guys came to seminars at the university. They were doing analyses of rare elements, but one man from G.A. became interested in doing aluminum in rocks. He may have heard us complain about how we had to do aluminum, which was by "difference." We did a group of elements—Ti, Fe, Al, and some remaining Si—then subtracted those values from the group, and aluminum was all of the rest of it. Naturally, this was our worst determination, so a lot of chemists became interested. They wanted to do aluminum directly, and that would be fine by me. They asked for some samples to take back to G.A. to irradiate with their atomic pile and count and then give us, finally, a very good analysis for aluminum. I was intrigued.

I gave them two samples, G-1 (granite) and W-1 (gabbro), which would have the composition of basalt. G-1 had about 14 percent aluminum and W-1 about 13 percent. There was enough aluminum in the rocks that they couldn't miss it. Silence for several months and then they returned—two men with two analyses. I was sitting on the end of my chair—all excited. Finally, I would know how much aluminum was really in these two standard rocks that had been sent to labs around the world. I can't remember exactly what they came up with, but G-1, they said, had about 1.3 weight percent aluminum and W-1 about 1.1 weight percent.

"Are you certain?"

"Yes."

"Wait. Do you have the decimal point in the wrong place?"

"No, we are certain of our numbers," they said.

Well, I could find more aluminum than they had by just sweeping the floor. We were very near the beach, and sand with aluminum-bearing feldspars came in on everyone's shoes. I spent half my time fighting to keep people with dirty feet out of the lab. I gave them the book with all the analyses of G-1 and W-1 made worldwide. They were so far off that they became angry with me.

"Look," I said, "I wanted it to work. I would have been delighted."

That was the end of neutron activation for analysis of aluminum. The men didn't come back again. That was the end of neutron activation for me. Besides, I don't have an atomic pile of my own.

Grand Canyon

Al decided that he had to have samples of Precambrian rock from the bottom of the Grand Canyon. Since the rocks of the Grand Canyon are like a layer cake, the oldest rocks, the Precambrian rocks, are exposed at the bottom of the canyon. I had never had a glimpse of the canyon, even though we drove by it about one hundred times on the way to somewhere else. We were always in such a hurry that we couldn't stop.

Now Al planned to do the trip right. We would have mules, a guide, and an extra mule to carry large samples of rock back to the rim of the canyon. It seems to me that people should not collect samples from the rocks of the canyon. The National Park Service must have rules now, but in those days park officials were fairly lenient.

I don't like to ride horses or mules, especially down narrow canyon trails, but the guide assured me that these mules were trained as pack animals for seven years before they took people to the bottom of the canyon. Instead of going down the Bright Angel Trail, which is customary, we were going down the Kaibab Trail, which is shorter and much steeper. The saddles on the mules were tied under the animal's belly, and another belt went around its bottom under the tail. The guide said that mules don't have shoulders like horses, so they had to cinch them up under the tail. The real reason was that the trail down was so steep that the saddle would fall off the animal, with the rider ending up in a thousand-foot fall.

They had me ride along in the rear.

"Don't let the mule graze on anything. Keep its head up. Let the animal go at its own pace. Don't rush the mule," said the guide.

Did this guy think that I would hurry the mule down this trail? I decided to pretend that I was composed of sacks of onions and potatoes. Mules are pack animals and can't tell if they are carrying food or people.

We started at what I would call a fairly brisk pace, but then we slowed to a crawl. The trail went along the cliff edge of beds of sedimentary rock. If the rider fell off in some parts of the trail, it would have been a free-fall for two thousand feet—perfect site for a hang glider to take off from. On the steep switchbacks, the mules are careful, but rocks slip under their feet and my mule, dammit, kept trying to nibble on small clumps of dried grass here and there. The mule knew I couldn't ride.

"Get that mule's head up."

"Yes, sir."

Across the canyon we could see for perhaps sixty

miles. On the steep switchbacks, I closed my eyes when the animal came very close to the edge. We stopped at one place to see the footprints of a small dinosaur preserved in the sedimentary rocks. That was very exciting. The footprints were of a small turkey-sized creature that had run across wet mud in a riverbed over 80 million years ago. Then the next layer of clay had covered the tracks. It was delightful to see the tracks of such an ancient animal, but also eerie. The tracks were so well preserved that they looked fresh. We were lucky that the beds of sedimentary rock split at this place so that we could see them. We must have been about one-third of the way down the canyon.

My knees began to hurt. First I thought the stirrups were too short.

I asked, "Are these stirrups too . . . ?"

"No, they are just right," the guide said.

I thought, *You have to relax, because you are killing your legs. Loosen up. Try to go limp.*

We came to a fascinating area in the old Precambrian sedimentary rocks where there were colonies of fossil algae preserved. These rocks were over 1,000 million years old. A sign read: Oldest Known Life. We photographed each other in front of the sign. Oh, it felt good to get off the mule.

"I am going to walk the rest of the way down, because this riding hurts my knees too much." The guide was disgusted with me. Horsemen, mulemen, always sneer at people who aren't stuck to a horse or a pickup. Al didn't say anything. He just took the reins of my mule and led it along behind his.

"Okay, you walk, but it is really stupid when you have paid to ride a mule," said the guide.

In those days the Phantom Ranch Lodge at the bottom of the canyon consisted of little stone and log cabins and a dining hall. Naturally, the mule riders arrived at the lodge before I did. In the bottom of the canyon, the weather was like late springtime, warm—with many deciduous trees leafed out in yellow-green. From late winter to spring in one agonizing day on and off a mule—from yesterday to 1,500 million years of geologic time. The Precambrian rocks at the bottom of the canyon are metamorphic rocks injected by dikes and sills of various igneous rocks. Here the canyon walls were almost vertical. It is called the Inner Gorge.

I can't remember many folks at the dining table except the man next to me. He had dieted for five years to get under two-hundred pounds. That is the maximum weight that the mules are allowed to carry, whether it is food, diesel fuel to run the generators, people, or supplies. This man on my left said his knees hurt, too, and he didn't know if he could get out of the canyon. Oh, Lord, what if I couldn't get out of here either? People came from all over the world to make this trip. This guy next to me and I wouldn't be able to get back up.

The next day, we had the guide and mules and we rode for maybe a mile north on Bright Angel Creek to collect the damned rocks. Al wanted samples of "red rock" formed along the edge of intrusions of igneous rock. Everyone thought, at that time, that the red rock was the chilled facies of the igneous intrusions and would represent the composition of the intrusions. I didn't care what it was at the time.

My knees hurt more than ever, and I walked back to the camp again. It wasn't a complete loss, because now Al had his rocks. I was beginning to wonder if a helicopter ever came down to the bottom to help the souls who couldn't get out. We were about one mile vertically below the rim of the canyon. I felt as old as the rocks.

The next night at dinner there was a new crowd of people. The man with the sore knees was gone. He got out someway or shot himself.

We went to sleep again. Tomorrow we would have to ride out. I must have slept for about three hours, and then I was wide awake. It was two o'clock in the morning.

"Al, I am going to get up now and try to walk out. I can't ride on that mule. I am crippled."

"Just go back to sleep. You can make it."

The next morning, we got on the mules again. I could tell the guide thought I was a big pain and not in the knees. I did ride as far as possible, maybe one-third of the way up. Then I had to get off and hobble the rest of the way. Al and the guide arrived at the top of the canyon hours before I finally made it. Al was at the end of the trail sort of looking for me. Perhaps he was hoping that vultures were feeding on my body. On the other hand, he still needed someone to do chemical analyses of the rocks, help raise the children, cook, and wash clothes.

I was in such bad shape that I couldn't pull my foot up to take off my shoes. I was such a damned mess that if I had been a horse, they would have shot me to get me out of my misery.

The next evening we planned to stay at a motel in Holbrook, Arizona, or some little town along the highway back to California. First we had to walk across the highway to get to a café to eat dinner. I could walk about as fast as a snail.

Al said, "We have to get across the highway before we are hit by a car."

He did stay with me, and I hung onto his arm. Then we got to the curb on the other side of the road. I had to stand in the gutter and try to get enough courage to step up on the curb. Al kept urging me and I finally made it up onto the curb.

Seeing the Grand Canyon from the rim is one of the most spectucular sights in the United States. When you think that a stream of water cut that immense canyon, you realize the erosive force of flowing water. The Colorado River carries a lot of sand and silt, and the water, plus sand, carved the canyon.

All the misery was worth it. I don't want to see it again, but I would urge everyone to see it once. But I could not recommend a mule ride to the bottom.

We became preoccupied with another project and never did work on the rocks. Al may have used some of them for teaching samples, but most lie quietly in trays in a basement storeroom.

The Henry Mountains

I was instructed to meet a geological party in Grand Junction, Colorado. The field station there was the main storage depot for the Atomic Energy Commission, and from there any geologic party was just a day away from uranium deposits in Utah.

My husband came from Denver with the other geologists involved. I started from Pasadena alone, in our GMC Carryall. We planned to sleep in the carryall because there were no motels in the Henry Mountains of Utah, where we planned to work.

I had to stay somewhere in Utah on the first night. After the interrogation I had from the female manager, you would think that I could remember the town, but I can't. I had been driving all day in low desert, hot desert, and high desert of California and Utah—miles and miles of desert with an occasional higher elevation where some juniper and pinion pines grew. I did get into a tiny rainstorm on a mountain pass and almost wrecked the vehicle. The road was slightly wet and corduroyed, and the Carryall started to fishtail. You need weight in the back to keep trucks from sliding sideways. Also, you must slow down.

The manager of the motel was a real pain.

"You are alone?"

"Yes."

"Why?"

"I am going to Grand Junction to join some government geologists."

"Alone?"

"Yes, alone. I can't drive all night, I am tired." I don't know what she thought I was—a gun moll, a traveling prostitute, or a Mormon woman trying to escape from Utah.

Women are their own worst enemies. I have known that all my life.

So I did arrive in Grand Junction, and there was the rest of the party—four men in a brand new Jeep. The Jeep was large enough to get us all in, crushed together, to be sure, but it would have been possible. However, I followed in the GMC. We backtracked west to Green River, Utah, and then went south to Hanksville, Utah.

In 1956 Hanksville, Utah, was the lost end of the world. It was almost a ghost town. Charlie Hunt, our field geologist, knew all the people in town, and the Ekkers were the first family. There was a grocery store and a post office, and we were able to buy gasoline, probably from the Ekkers. The population of Hanksville was about twenty-five souls.

Charles B. Hunt was in charge of this field expedition. He is truly a remarkable geologist. He tackled jobs no one else would touch, and he always finished and did a superb study. Of course, his work took years to complete, and the regions he chose to work on were often remote and always enormous. There are few geologists like him in the United States. When Hunt started in the Henry Mountains, he had to build some of the roads and Jeep trails through sandy and rocky slopes and stream beds. I guess the early road was a horse and cattle trail. The topographic maps, which geologists need to record data, were old and in a very large scale. Hunt had to make his own base maps, too. Then he started interpreting the geologic features. This area of Utah extended from Green River to Hanksville, south to the Colorado River, and east to Moab. It had not been mapped since Powell, another adventuresome geologist, looked at the area in the nineteenth century. The last people there were the Ute Indians, who, according to Powell's notes, were also watching him, and the Utes were not friendly. Powell was fearless and dedicated, and the Indians didn't harm him.

The area near Hanksville was first settled by white Mormon people, but they did not seem to prosper here. The soil was lean and the climate dry, so many moved on.

The Ekkers stayed, and they loved this lonely place. They were charming people. Hunt said they had offered us their bunkhouse in which to sleep. I can best describe the bunkhouse by saying that it had walls but no roof. This place was for summer company only, but it did offer some protection from the wind. There were quite a few metal cots with springs. Some of the men put their bedrolls on the cots. Al and I slept on the ground nearby.

It was warm and dry, and I must have forgotten about rattlesnakes crawling around at night.

The next day we started walking, and I mean WALKING. Charlie Hunt wanted to show us some curious types of granitic intrusions called laccoliths and bysmaliths. Granitic rocks intruded between layers of sedimentary beds had produced domical bulging in the overlying strata. Laccoliths form enormous blisters of igneous rock interlayered in the sediments. Bysmaliths are intrusions of granitic rock that rose vertically into the sediments and carried the layers of sediments on top like icing on a cake.

All the igneous rocks are porphyries, with large crystals of feldspar in a fine-grained matrix. This sort of texture is thought to be formed in magma intruded from a molten magma chamber near the surface. We could walk up to the contact of igneous rock with sediment, and the sediments were not baked or chemically altered and were only slightly discolored. These were relatively "cool" intrusions.

On the first day, at two in the afternoon, I became tired, bored, and hungry. I was crabbing to my husband, "Why are we walking all around this thing? We know what these structures are now and what has happened. When can we eat lunch? I am tired. I want to sit down."

He said, "Shut up."

We did finally sit down to eat mashed cucumber sandwiches next to a muddy little stream. Probably Hunt wanted us to get some idea of the scale of his work. After the first few exposures, I didn't need to see any more of the stuff up so close. I could see the whole area, and the structures were enormous.

When we were not walking, Hunt liked to take short cuts in the jeep. He would simply turn into the rocks and start to drive up or down the layers of rock. It was terrifying. The jeep fumed and fussed and scraped along, and it tilted at angles until I was certain the vehicle would roll over with us in it. We were just creeping along.

"I want to get out and walk behind," I whispered to my husband.

He said, "Shut up." Why is it a sign of weakness to want to live?

Most geologists are crazy. They let the chief of party call all the shots, and I think they would march over a cliff like lemmings if the leader did so. It was considered a sign of weakness if you objected or died in your tracks.

The Ekker men were smart and stayed in the camp. They always had a deer hanging for steaks, and they had sourdough rolls ready when we came in at night. Oh, the food tasted good. In the evening after a few drinks, they would tell about the country. One brother was the sheriff for half of southern Utah.

He said, "I hear there is a body down near the Colorado River, and I should try to get to it before winter." No sweat, laid back, piece of cake, guys.

They had a gold placer mine they could work only when the water was plentiful in the spring. Then when summer came they would lease it to some greenhorn. After three months of struggling as the creek went dry, that gold miner would be wiped out. There wasn't enough water for placer mining in the summer and fall. It takes quite a lot of water to wash gold out of gravel. Besides, the placer deposits didn't contain much gold.

Everybody laughed at and about their stories. Sometimes I felt sorry for the greenhorns.

One evening they said, "We need more deer meat. You come with us."

"Me?"

"Yes, you."

"I don't want to see you shoot a deer"—but I couldn't be a total wet blanket.

Then they pulled apart some bushes and out rumbled a U.S. Army half-track (I think it is called that)—a big, lumbering vehicle that chugged along on metal cleats and spouted black smoke.

I crawled in and hung on. We went up into the mountains on what must have been an old lumbering road. They said that when hunting season opened in the fall, they felled trees across this road so no one would come hunting here except them. Any of the brothers could have picked up a good-sized tree. They had a lot of guns along, and deer were everywhere. I was prepared to hold my ears and close my eyes when they shot.

Then the banter started.

"What do you think of that deer?"

"Naw, too small."

"How about that big buck?"

I held my ears.

"Naw, let him go".

"There's a big doe. Hell, no, she has two fawns." The talk went on and on as we went on and on grinding along on this bumpy road up the mountains.

Finally, we turned on a slight curve and there was a big buck lying there, very dead, with its tongue hanging out. "We'll take that one," they said. If they had told me that we were going to pick up the dead body of a deer they had shot in the late afternoon, I could have enjoyed the scenery and the live deer because I could have kept my eyes open.

In the summer they had garden vegetables, but they lived mostly on venison and sourdough rolls. Oh, and sourdough pancakes for breakfast with burnt sugar syrup. When we returned home, I tried to get a sourdough starter mix going, but it didn't work for me and it didn't taste as good as it did in the mountains.

Our party consisted of my boss, my husband, and a geochemist who was going to collect enough igneous rocks to extract zircons and date the age of the igneous rocks. I think I was there because my boss offered Hunt help on the general chemistry of the igneous rocks. Hunt didn't need me. He had enough of it done by chemists in Denver. Maybe I could add something to the petrographic study of thin sections and to the chemistry of the minerals in the igneous rocks, but not all that much.

We collected hundreds of pounds of diorite porphyry (igneous rock) for the geochemist, and that all went into the jeep, too. Then we went south down the Dirty Devil River to Hite, Utah. On the way, Hunt told us about a skeleton of a big dinosaur that was exposed nearby. Oh, I would loved to have seen that, but there wasn't time. There wasn't time to do the really fascinating things. A few little stores had huge thighbones of dinosaurs propped up outside to sell. I didn't get to look at those either—not enough time.

The road to Hite was red and dusty, and there were signs all along the way—Watch for Flash Floods. I kept looking back every time we crossed a low spot in the road, even though the sky was clear and the sun a ball of fire overhead.

Hite is underwater now, part of the damming projects on the Colorado River. To be specific, Hite is now under Lake Powell, but then it was a very small farming community and the few residents grew delicious melons. We stopped and bought some to eat. Now I was fussing about not being able to phone home to find out if our children were okay. My husband said, "You are going to lose your job." I shot back, "I don't care. If I can't find a telephone somewhere, I am just going home and you can't stop me."

"Oh, for God's sake, shut up," he said.

Remember what I told you? Women are their own worst enemies.

We crossed the Colorado River on a ferry. It looked scary. They had stretched a rusty, frayed metal cable across the river, and the ferry was a couple of planks powered by an old Cadillac engine. The engine pulled along the cable, pulling the ferry. The river was swift and muddy here and . . . "What if the cable breaks?" "Shut up."

We made it to Moab, home of the newly rich uranium miners and all the poor men who didn't find a thing. I saw a telephone sign and went for it. They had to wait for me for half an hour while the call was routed through Green River, Provo, Salt Lake City, and elsewhere and finally to Pasadena, California.

Our older son answered. He was about ten, I guess.
"How are you?"
"Fine."
"Oh, I was so worried."
"What for?"
"I'll be home very soon now."
"You don't have to hurry. We like being with Grandma better."
"Oh, shut up."

Silica Accumulator Project

My boss at the U.S. Geological Survey, Tom Lovering, had enormous enthusiasm and usually managed to dream up the most monstrous and bizarre projects. His latest idea stunned me. He wanted to test the possibility that plants could accumulate enough of a given element in the tissues that when the plants died, decomposed, and were washed away, a large concentration of another enriched element might be left behind in the soil and rock. In this instance, he wanted to try to test if specific plants could accumulate silica from soil/rock and through thousands of years, the extraction of silica from the soil by plants would leave a deposit of aluminum-rich clay (bauxite). Bauxite is the primary ore used to make aluminum ingots for your pop and beer cans, auto and airplane parts, and so on. And silicon and aluminum are the most abundant elements in rocks of the crust of the Earth.

Now we know that coal deposits form from plant materials but the process takes millions and millions of years. Lovering wanted to speed up a process that in nature would take a million or more years. We were to attempt to show clearly that depletion of soils of silica, leaving them enriched in aluminum, could be accomplished in several years. To do this, he wanted me to go to a plant laboratory, the Earhart Laboratory at Caltech, where we could modify all aspects of climate and attempt to test this idea. I was to present the project to the director of the plant laboratory, and we would pay for the space, so much per square foot, from the U.S. Geological Survey, in Denver, Colorado.

I don't care how long I lived, I knew I could not speed up the process to the end stage Tom wanted, but he insisted that we (I) try. I should have said no and hung up on him. But then he was my boss and he would have come to Pasadena himself and signed me up or fired me. Lovering had free use of FTS, the Federal Telecommunication System, so he could hang on the phone for days or call me anytime, night or day. He was very stubborn and proud of his pet ideas.

Professor Bonner ran the lab at Caltech, called the Phytatron. I was nervous speaking to him about this crazy project, but I must have made a decent presentation because Bonner said, "Okay." I was too stupid to be let out alone. I should have made a lousy presentation and made the project sound hopeless. That would have been easy. Then Bonner would have rejected the project and written us off as crackpots.

Incidentally, Bonner was raising various varieties of tomatoes for the Campbell Soup Company. He was trying for a more flavorful, darker red tomato. Of course, he had other projects, too, but I do remember the tomatoes. I even thought of picking and eating some of them when I was in the plant lab alone in the evening, but I didn't.

Then came all the rules in the plant laboratory. Everyone involved in the lab changed from their street clothes into clean white coats and cloth boots over the shoes. Did I have to cover my hair? I can't remember. They gave me a locker to store my street clothes. No cigarettes were allowed in the plant laboratory, because everyone was afraid of contaminating the place with the tobacco mozaic virus. (This was going on in the late 1950s, so I can't remember all of the do's and don'ts.)

Lovering wanted to grow *Arundu donax,* a giant bamboolike grass that did accumulate silica, and two other grasses. We decided to use alumina-rich basalt, rhyolite, and a granitic rock also enriched in aluminum. Then Lovering thought of another plant—*Equisetum hymale. Equisetum* is a favorite plant for geologists who are paleobotanists because forms of *Equisetum* have been around for a long time.

The project was going to take a lot of rock to fill ninety-six plastic flowerpots. Each pot was large, about six liters. Tom had other plants and other rocks he wanted to try, but I was able to cool him down to four plants and three rock types. This was an enormous project, and I had no enthusiasm for it at all.

We went to the desert east of Pasadena to find a basaltic volcano with a lot of aluminum in the rock. Not a live volcano, naturally, but a dead one. The Santa Fe Railroad owned land with a neat volcanic cone of basalt—Pisgah Crater. The railroad used the crackled basaltic cinders on their railroad bed. My husband helped me and we shoveled up a half-truckload of basaltic cinders. First, I had to ask permission at the railroad yard.

"Sure," the manager said, "take all you want. Just leave us enough for the railroad." Uh, he was trying to be funny.

It was all black rock and hot and windy out there in the desert. We took along a geologist from England, who was interested in recent basaltic volcanoes. At least he liked the trip, but his wife came along and said that this was a horrible place. Then she launched into a tirade about all the terrible places she had been with her husband. I listened. Did she think I didn't know about the terrible places that geologists go?

We went to the Sidewinder Well Road, near Barstow, California, for the rhyolite. No one cared how much of that rock we carried away. Certainly the sidewinder rattlesnakes didn't care.

Then we used the Peninsular Range granitic rocks. We found a place where the rock was disintegrated into a coarse sand. That was the "granitic" rock, a quartz diorite.

I can't remember all of the details. I have spent years trying to forget the whole project.

To begin, I had to analyze these rocks carefully for a lot of major elements, particularly for silicon, aluminum, calcium, sodium, potassium, and iron. The trace elements were done in the Denver Laboratory.

Then what to feed these plants because they would not grow in sterile rock? The basalt was a much better growing medium for the plants than the granite, but still needed nutrients. We used the standard fertilizer used in the lab, which was chemicals put directly into the water. So during the watering the plants were fertilized. I planned to catch all of the water and recycle it through the pots. I had plastic tubes attached to the holes in the bottom of the pots. These drained into large polyethylene bottles. I asked the people at the Phytaron not to water my plants. I put red flags on my plants so that no one could miss them, but a lot of weekend workers poured the fertilized water all over everything with a pressurized hose. The experiment was falling apart already.

Naturally, all materials that went into the Phytatron lab had to be sterilized to prevent infections from outside. The laboratory had a chute for all nonsterile materials. We put everything—rocks, pots, labels, and plants—into large canvas bags and put the bags into the chute. Two days later, all of the stuff arrived inside the lab, sterilized. The plants were a mess. I did not think they would ever recover.

I planted the *Arundu,* and the damned plants recovered and grew into big, lush plants. They almost grew to the roof. Of course, this plant lab had controlled humidity, temperature, sunlight, water, and fertilizer. It was a plant heaven. Everyone had interesting projects in there, all sorts of orchids and other tropical beauties that I didn't know. The lab had a delightful odor with the perfume from flowers and all that extra oxygen trapped inside for us to breathe. And all I had were those giant grasses. The *Equisetum* plants would not grow in the warmer greenhouse (seventy-five degrees Fahrenheit). They had to be transferred to a cooler section of the Phytaron. More work.

I gave up on the rocks. Too many odd chemicals were circulated through the crushed rocks and it became impossible to keep track of the data. We were not in the computer age. I don't think computers could have helped me anyway. Besides, I had such a poor attitude. However, we could study what the plants were accumulating, if anything. I cut bunches and bunches of *Arundu* and *Equisetum* and took them to my laboratory. After drying them in an oven, I tried to turn the remainder into ash, so that I could analyze that. The ash was so light and fluffy that I couldn't handle it at all, and I needed a lot of ash to make an analysis.

After several years of struggling, I handed all the pages of analyses and related data back to Lovering, hoping that the statistical problems would frustrate even him. Splits of the rocks and bundles of grasses and *Equisetum* were mailed to him. I did not hear a peep from Lovering for a long while. Just as I was about to forget the whole project, page proofs of a large article discussing the project arrived for me to look at. I was aghast. "Do not put my name on this paper," I asked and I pleaded. "You have done all the thinking." I was calling on the FTS system now, and I was trying to be polite. But the published paper is out there somewhere, and I am a coauthor and ashamed of it. There are many similar screwy and inaccurate projects published as "science." When scientists fall in love with their ideas, they lose the ability to test them.

That happens to politicians, too.

Scripps

We hated to leave Caltech, but the smog in the Los Angeles Basin and east to Riverside became intolerable. Al liked to work outside on weekends. He always had giant projects going—great concrete walls, stairways of brick, and his favorite project, digging trenches and laying pipes for sprinkling systems. Albert should have been a master plumber. Our younger son, Tom, liked to play with all the tools. Tom was quiet for several hours one Saturday morning, and then I heard all this shrieking by Albert. Tom had sawed off the handles of Al's metal pipe-threader. That is a difficult job for a little kid to do with a hacksaw.

When Al worked outside in the smog, he started to cough a lot. He didn't smoke. His cough couldn't be from cigarettes. We thought of trying to commute from a home near the ocean where the smog was not as thick. We travelled all of the coastline from north to south hoping to find a different home. Every place was too far away. Besides, Al hated to drive.

Then a position became available at the Scripps Institution of Oceanography in La Jolla, California. We could both work there, and they were building new laboratories. We got in early enough that we could help design the lab. That was fun.

Al took a year's leave-of-absence, and we built a home in Del Mar near the institute. I had to commute back to the lab at Caltech in order to keep my chemical work going. Fortunately, Bill Menard was driving to Caltech every Monday and returning to La Jolla on Thursday or Friday. He let me drive along with him.

Later, Bill Menard would be called an oceanographer. When I first knew him, he was interested in land forms above water—a geomorphologist. We used to drive along the coastal highway counting old beach terraces, and we wondered if the land was rising or the ocean shrinking. Menard was a very wealthy man, but he was frugal. The graduate students brought beer to sell at the seminars on Thursday night. Menard had a beer in his hand, and when I sat down next to him, he reached into his pocket for a quarter. I thought he was going to buy a beer for me. Then he pulled his hand back and decided not to waste twenty-five cents on me. I don't like beer anyway. It is absurd—the things that people remember about other people.

I didn't like Scripps as well as Caltech. There were more geologists at Caltech and geologists are usually more fun than chemists and physicists. Biologists and geologists who are working out-of-doors don't take themselves as seriously as other scientists. That is just one observation from one female.

We had lunch one day with Roger Revelle, director of Scripps, and Revelle suggested that he wanted us to study the rocks of the Hawaiian Islands. Al became all bristly about that. He didn't want to be told about what kind of geological work to do. However, I was thinking, *I may finally get to Hawaii.* Everyone wants to see Hawaii, at least once. Revelle didn't know that about two hundred geologists and chemists were working on lava flows of the Hawaiian Islands. We didn't think about Hawaii again.

Prof. Carl Hubbs was organizing a biological expedition to Guadalupe Island, off Mexico. They were going to capture some elephant seals, count whales and seals, and do other biological experiments.

Al and I thought that maybe we could go together and get ashore each day from the ship to map and collect rocks—all volcanic rocks—(lava flows, pyroclastics, tuff, pumice, volcanic bombs, green clots of olivine) a cornucopia of rock types. Al and I went to the dock in San Diego to look at the ship together. It was named *Horizon*. The ship looked small to me, but I think it was the largest ship in the fleet at the time. They had at least three ships that were smaller than *Horizon*.

We asked a man on board where we would sleep. He took us below the deck into a tiny dark room with two bunks. The air was warm and fetid in the cabin. The mattresses smelled. The whole lower deck was rancid. Probably World War II submarines would smell better than this tub.

I said, "I AM NOT GOING."

"You should go. What am I going to tell them if you don't go?" Al said.

"I don't care what you tell them. Tell them it stinks." I would only be caught dead in that cabin below deck, and then I wouldn't care.

Al went on the trip and collected a wonderful group of volcanic rocks. We worked on the mineralogy and chemistry of this volcanic island and used the data to evaluate other volcanic islands in the Pacific. I was beginning to learn a lot about volcanic rocks.

I don't think that Al minds being in a smelly bed or wearing dirty clothes, at least not when he has interesting rocks to look at. All field geologists were like that three generations back. Al and I began to notice, however, that the younger generation of field geologists were not like that. They found it difficult to work alone. They needed "noise" and people around them. Field geologists may disappear for several reasons. Fieldwork takes lots of time and is physically demanding. You could work years to get one good map and scientific paper. Then too, in a lot of areas in the world, millions of people have covered rock exposures with houses and moved rocks away to plant fields of food. The most barren deserts, highest mountains and coldest regions may be all that is left to study, and those areas will be too "lonely."

In the sixties and seventies at Scripps and on to today, science changed a great deal. Then everyone was scratching around for money for everything. You couldn't mail a letter or have a telephone unless you have a grant from ONR, NSF, NIH, or a private foundation. Sometimes taxpayers complained to me that they didn't want to fund a university in their state. Now state universities are lucky to get a few dollars from each state tax bill. Most of the money must come from proposals made by each university member to some arm of the federal government or a private foundation or company. Now there are more scientists, chasing less and less money.

At Scripps, the Office of Naval Research had a death grip on the institute. I sat in on one meeting when the navy men came to call. The navy wanted maps—shoreline maps, topographic maps, maps and more maps. And if you could sail into the Sea of Okhotsk or anywhere near the Soviet Union, you could get all the money you needed. The U.S. Navy didn't give a damn if the Soviets shot you out of the water. Fortunately, the National Science Foundation took over the Deep-Sea Drilling Project, or we wouldn't know a thing about the crust of the ocean. The crust of the ocean covers about two-thirds of the Earth's surface.

And the CIA showed up. Al was going to the Soviet Union to give a talk on the composition of the oceanic crust. This operative showed up and asked Al to take photos of Soviet scientists.

"Don't you do that!" I screamed, "Don't even think about it. If you are caught, you will be in Siberia forever." Al is not a good liar. Anyone can tell he is lying when he tries it. He couldn't possibly be a spy. He would show everyone that he was spying.

Professor Goldberg came into our lab almost daily. He would rush into the room, discuss something with Al, and then slide out the door and slam it. Everything on the lab benches rattled, including my delicate balance. Wouldn't a good chemist like Goldberg know better than to slam the door? I could forgive Ed because he told a lot of funny jokes at lunch. I had a slice of raisin bread one day in my lunch bag. Goldberg swatted a fly with his hand and tossed it toward me and told me to put it in with the other raisins.

Jenny and Gustav Arrhenius built a beautiful home high on a bluff facing out to sea. Of course, I remember the view, which was stunning, and the rugs on the floor, which were hand woven in blues and greens and came from Sweden. Everything was elegant. On the windowsills and cabinets was an array of pottery. It looked familiar to me. No wonder. All of this ancient pottery came from Mesa Verde Monument in the United States. One of their relatives had excavated and collected from Mesa Verde before the U.S. had sense enough to do it. At least some of it came back from Sweden to the United States with Gus and Jenny.

The Raitts built a home with a sea view also. The house sort of rambled around on the top of a cliff. They had a guest house attached, and many foreign scientists stayed with them from time to time. Helen Raitt kept a marvelously cluttered house. I always felt at home there. Russ Raitt had a house and car in the desert near Borrego Springs. The car was a two-cylinder Citroen with front-wheel drive. I was impressed with that vehicle. Russ took off the doors, and then we would race around in the sand of the desert looking for recent fault scarps. We had two large earthquakes in two years, and Russ was always able to find the surface trace of the fault zone. However, he didn't let me drive that car, because it was his baby. One hot day we were miles from water or help and the engine started to sputter. "What are we going to do?" I asked.

"Oh, don't worry, I have paper clips and rubber bands along," Russ said. Of course, he carried more substanial tools and he was able to fix that little auto. One year he went to France and bought another Citroen just like the first. Then he would have spare parts for one whole car.

I remember a lot of Al's students because they came into the laboratory and pestered me for help and equipment. My favorite student was Alan Divis. He was the kind of guy everyone needs. He could pick the locks on the secretaries' cars when they locked themselves out. He held his baby in one arm while he wrote scientific papers with his free arm. Alan could do everything from sophisticated mathematics to overhauling the engine of his car. He knew he was very sharp, and he didn't hide it. He was going to Denver to work in the chemical labs of the Geological Survey. His mother loaned him her car so that he could drive to Denver and get around there. When he came back to Scripps, he was crabbing about his mother's car. It didn't have enough power. That is when I attacked him. He was fussing around about mothers, and I was a mother. Alan had another aggravating habit. He would come into the lab to talk with me or anyone, and then he would start looking at his wristwatch—about every two minutes. I should have warned him to hide his intellect—just a little—and stop looking at his wristwatch.

Basalts

Al and I were sitting in the room where we stored all of our Precambrian rock specimens. All of these rocks were over 1,000 million years old. We were looking at thin sections of metamorphic rocks through our polarizing microscope. We were facing a wall, but we could see the hall, too.

Dr. Bill Riedel was walking down the hall with a wooden tray of rocks. It looked heavy. Riedel stopped and visited for a while.

"What do you have in the tray?"

Riedel said, "These are igneous rocks, basalts, which have been dredged from the ocean floor by Scripps ships at various locations."

"Oh, please let us look at them."

So Riedel came in and placed the tray on a table. Some rocks had thin sections lying beside the samples.

"We would like to look at the thin sections," I said.

"Okay, you can have them," he said.

"To keep?"

"Yes."

After Riedel was gone, Al said, "Who would want to study basalts?"

That statement from Al—after we looked at the samples, we studied basalts from the ocean floor for over eight years.

Most of the rocks in the tray were quite altered, but a few were relatively fresh. At about this time, the National Science Foundation and several universities were talking about drilling deep into the ocean floor to find out what was below the blanket of sediments.

They had to get and outfit a ship that was able to buck winds and currents to stay centered over a deep drill hole. They had to recover rock and reenter the hole, adding pipe and drill stem to drill deeper. And they wanted to recover all of the rock or as much as possible. Nobody knew for sure what rocks were down there. The problem is that most of the oceans are well over ten thousand feet deep. So they had to lower two to three miles of pipe and drill stem through water before they could start drilling into the seafloor. Big problems. Engineers were everywhere. I don't remember a lot about the first ship except it was designed for drilling for oil in offshore waters. It had motors positioned to try to keep the ship over the same position even in windy weather. Actually, it was a drilling barge that had to be towed to the sites. It was named *Cuss I*.

Later they built a ship that was much more stable than this one, with the motors and propeller speeds controlled by computer. The new ship was very effective and has drilled in all the oceans.

An interesting sideline—this new ship and a sister ship were built by the navy to drag up a sunken Russian submarine. This was all hush-hush, but later it came out in various newspapers and magazines. They only recovered small parts of the submarine and nothing very useful. Why do we spend so much time and money trying to watch and outwit the Russians?

One of the first drilling sites was near 28°58' North, 117°28' West, and was called the Guadalupe Site. The ocean there was about 11,700 feet deep (3,566 meters). It was south, southwest of Scripps, almost at our back door.

The drilling was a success, and they recovered quite a bit of basalt. The basalts drilled from this site were labelled EM for Experimental Mohole. The word *Mohole* is a short version of *Mohorovicic Discontinuity*. I don't want to try to explain that here except to say that the ocean crust is relatively thin, only four to seven miles thick. We know from all sorts of studies using elastic waves created by earthquakes that the rocks beneath the oceanic crust, in the mantle, are very different from those in the ocean crust. In the beginning they were going to try to drill through the ocean crust to the mantle below. Rocks in the mantle are thought to be enriched in magnesium and iron—very different from the rocks of the ocean crust. They didn't get to drill to the mantle. It would have been too costly, the techniques did not exist, and Congress would not approve the expense.

Lots of jokes and stories were made up about drilling into the mantle, which might be HOT. One I recall was in the form of a driller's log. It was a small booklet with drilling data, date, depth to bottom each day, rock type, and so forth. The last pages were scorched around the edges as the drillers described their last days on the drilling platform. Then they fled and the final page was burned and crinkled. The drill stem melted and the drilling platform blew up. It was funny and in more detail than I have described here. I should have tried to get a copy.

When the drillers on the ship at the EM site finally hit basalt, the cursing started. Basalt is a very hard rock. Drilling into it destroyed the drill bits. At first they could only core about one foot or less per day. After weeks of work, they finally solved the problem of drilling basalts. They designed better drill bits and stronger motors to spin the bit, but it was never easy. Engineers worked night and day because the scientists were clamoring for more complete and longer cores.

When the drill at the Guadalupe Site bottomed in basalt, we asked for samples, please, so we could analyze the rock for the elements that would tell us most about the kind of basalt. They gave us a piece of the core that was about fifteen centimeters long and roughly six centimeters in diameter. It was an altered basalt with veins of calcium carbonate and other alteration materials, but we were able to saw out a fairly fresh piece that was big enough for our work.

To make a long story short, the basalt cored from the ocean bottom had very low amounts of K (potassium). Al and I wrote a short paper that compared this cored basalt with basalts from the Hawaiian Islands, Deccan (India), and the Columbia River. They were similar, but all of the land basalts had higher amounts of potassium. I should have caught on immediately. I did the potassium on a flame photometer, and the K was so low that I had to make up more and more standards with lower amounts of K. The best sample of basalt had a potassium content of 0.10 weight percent. I dismissed it as an oddball, an altered basalt. By then, I had at least four new standard solutions for potassium: 0.20, 0.10, and two I didn't trust, at 0.05 and 0.01 weight percent. Our distilled water was not that pure.

In the meantime, we were working on basalts from the wooden tray and new dredge hauls from the East Pacific Rise.

Dr. Gustaf Arrenhius came in one day with a gorgeous sample of glassy black basalt from the East Pacific Rise. One of his buddies had dredged it several weeks before, and someone had carried it by air to San Diego after the ship docked in Tahiti.

Gus said, "This is a rhyolite [granitic composition] from the East Pacific Rise." Granitic rocks were not supposed to occur in the deep oceans. I could hardly keep my hands off it. How come a woman could get excited about a shiny black rock? A big emerald, yes, but this rock?

"No, Gus, this is not a rhyolite. Pick it up and note how heavy it is. It contains a lot of iron. It is a basalt."

"No, it's a rhyolite."

"It's a basalt." Stubborn, both of us.

"Well, if you are certain it is a basalt, then I don't want it," Gus said.

"I'll take it. Thank you very much." Oh, I had it in my hands. It was a beauty from another part of the oceans.

It was one of our prized samples. It was part of a basaltic "pillow" from a site where the great Pacific rock plates were being pulled apart. The lava erupted and flowed out onto the ocean floor as a series of rounded globs and the cold water froze them. In addition, one of the staff had taken beautiful photos of the ocean bottom showing ripple-marked sand and many pillows of fresh basalt. These rocks and several other basalts were collected on Expedition Amphitrite. (Each expedition had a name.)

All of the basalts had very low amounts of potassium, from about ten to twenty thousand parts of K in a million parts of rock. The element potassium is radioactive and closely related to all the other radioactive elements in the earth, such as U (uranium) and Rb (rubidium). These and other large cations are critical to understanding why the earth quakes, erupts, and rarely sleeps.

Everybody was excited. If the ocean floor basalts covering over two-thirds of the earth were low in K, U, Rb, and so on, it meant that the earth was not as radioactive as was thought.

Colleagues in Denver at the U.S. Geological Survey

did Ba (barium), Pb (lead), and Th (thorium) counts, and they were low, too. Then they convened a conference at Scripps. Al was not in town, but I sat in the conference, in back, way in the back, to hear what they would say.

Some of the geochemists were rude. They talked to each other in the front row while others were speaking. One said, "I have to have some samples of these basalts because I don't believe her potassium numbers are correct. She's wrong." I'm wrong? Others attacked the Ba (barium) values. I did not say a word, but I was swayed by these powerhouse geochemists. Maybe I was wrong. How did I mess up? "We want your samples," they said, and we sent samples to many universities in the U.S. and Canada.

Finally, I got more dredge hauls from the Indian Ocean from Expedition Dodo. Each expedition had several goals: to core for sediments, dredge for hard rocks, collect deepwater animals, collect water samples from the surface and deeper, check heat flow from the earth with a probe, put out arrays of sonobouys for geophysicists, and more.

Basalts from the Indian Ocean were not so fresh and beautiful, but the K (potassium) was low, too. We were now pouring out small papers on each ocean, and Bob Fisher joined us on this work in the Indian Ocean. He knew the Indian Ocean well. He dredged a lot, and he was planning to go back again and dredge some more.

Professor Vacquier brought some dredged basalts from the south Atlantic Ocean—not many, three, as I recall. He said he didn't want to be on a paper because he didn't know a thing about rocks. He is a geophysicist. Thank you for the rocks, Vacquier.

Then I found an analysis published by the British of

a sample of basalt from the Carlsberg Ridge in the Indian Ocean. The chemistry of their basalt was the same as ours. This unique basalt seemed to be the principal igneous rock in the crust of the oceans.

Al was out dredging in the South Pacific, trying for basalts farther to the west, from both the ocean floor and from submarine volcanoes. While he was gone, I worked a lot at night. After I fed the grown sons, now in high school, I went back to work. A woman's work is never done. I am not complaining. I liked the work. Always, I was able to worry on several levels. Would the police call and tell me one or the other of our sons was dead on the highway? What should we have for dinner? Did I turn off the stove when I left in the morning? Was the iron on? In the lab, I did most of my extra worrying while I was looking at thin sections of rock through the microscope. This is a sort of quiet time, and if you know the rocks, your mind can wander about. I noticed that Al could worry about, at most, one thing at a time and his worries were different than mine.

One evening a colleague, Dr. Manny Bass, came into the lab. I enjoyed visiting with him. I couldn't leave the inner lab—too much stuff was boiling and steaming—so he came in and put down a manuscript that he had been asked to read. It was from a British geologist and contained a table of chemical analyses of basalts from the Mid-Atlantic Ridge from twenty-two to fifty-two degrees north, four samples, from different locations.

Bass asked me why the alumina was so high in the analyses of basalts (either mistakes in analyses or from an abundance of aluminum-rich feldspars in the lavas), but my eyes were riveted on the potassium. K was very low. That settled it for me. The basalts from the deep oceans were distinctly different than basalts from the continents, but we had only thirty-six samples in all the world oceans.

Bass said, "Would you like to take the manuscript home and comment on it?"

"NO, no thank you."

We had it. The basalts of the world oceans were unique basalts depleted in all the large cations. I was out of my mind with excitement.

I put all the data we had on the oceans in tables and graphs. Then I took the data to Al's study—a huge mess where he worked at night—and told him to have a rough draft of a manuscript by the end of the week and to keep it short and to the point. He could write ten pages on almost any little thing.

The geochemists who said I was wrong about the numbers for potassium in these basalts checked everything and duplicated my numbers, but they never apologized for saying, "She is wrong."

Crossings

After working in the laboratory on these basalts from the oceans, I was going to join an expedition at sea. I was to meet a Scripps ship, the *Argo,* in the Indian Ocean.

I requested permission to join the expedition, which was almost two years in the future. I phoned my boss in Menlo Park at the U.S. Geological Survey and presented the project to him and asked if I could join the expedition at Mauritius.

"Where?"

"It is an island in the Indian Ocean east of Madagascar." I had to get out an atlas to find it myself.

"Well, write up some sort of proposal so we can talk about it here."

"Thank you, I will." I planned to go even if they said no, but they said yes, I could go.

I didn't have to think about it immediately, it was planned so far in advance. I said that I would go along and then forgot about it.

But a year and many months went by and I had an airline ticket to London and on to islands in the Indian Ocean and I was afraid to get packed. In two weeks I would have to leave, so I opened a suitcase on our bedroom floor and started putting stuff into the suitcase. I was having a lot of second and third thoughts. The Indian Ocean was far from home, about halfway around the world and down under, and I was not a good long-distance traveler. I was a frightened airplane passenger at first but after I boarded the plane, I was fine. It sounds so ridiculous; I still don't like to fly. Our older son said it isn't natural to drive a car on a crowded freeway either.

I asked everyone who would listen, "Should I go on this trip?" Everyone said, "Well, certainly." Then I was forced to do something—go or unpack the suitcase.

In a burst of enthusiasm, I upgraded my ticket to London to first-class. If I were to get across the Atlantic Ocean, it might as well be first-class. Sixteen years ago, it was not very costly to go first-class. My dear grandmother crossed the Atlantic at age fifteen in steerage, alone, and here I was afraid to cross. I wonder what I thought would be so different in first-class. It would be quiet and have more room, more food, and more liquor—I don't drink much anyway.

I bought some new clothes. One item was a London Fog raincoat, which I liked very much. I had it over my shoulders on the flight from San Diego to Los Angeles. When I got out of the seat in Los Angeles, I forgot to pick up the coat. Damn, I was younger then and already I was forgetting important items. There was a two-hour waiting period in the Los Angeles airport, and there I lost my cosmetic case. There was nothing very important in the case, but now I didn't have my lipstick, comb, face cream, or toothbrush—or my coat. I still had my ticket, purse, and passport and a suitcase in baggage. The great wonder is that the suitcase traveled with me all the way to the Indian Ocean.

Before dark, the airplane flew on a course over the eastern part of the Canadian Shield. The terrain is quite flat and composed of old Precambrian rocks that have been scoured by glaciers. Many of the lakes and rivers were aligned north-south. When the continental glaciers flowed south, they gouged out furrows that turned into lakes—lots of lakes all over the land. I watched until darkness fell. A geologist can always find a rock or a landform to look at.

It is lovely to sit in first-class, and there is a lot more room for legs and body. A stewardess put me in a window seat, starboard, the last seat in first-class, with no one behind me. She said it would be quiet there. She didn't have anyone sit next to me. How did I know that she planned to have various members of the flight crew sit in the seat next to me all night long?

Dinner was delicious, with a choice of entree. I ate everything, but I couldn't drink all those cocktails, wines, and after-dinner drinks. What a shame, a waste, really, but the other passengers drank their share and all of mine. Then they quieted down and fell asleep and I was wide awake.

The cabin door opened, and a young man came out.

Did they have a navigator in those days? Well, anyway, he was the youngest crew member. He plopped down in the seat next to me, lowered his seat back as far as possible, and fell asleep immediately, and he snored. It wasn't all that objectionable, and since I wasn't sleeping, it didn't matter, but I was nervous. If I moved, would he wake up? I wanted him to get all the rest he needed. After all, he was part of the crew that was flying this airplane. TWA? Pan Am? I can't remember which airline that was, but we always tried to fly on an American carrier. The National Science Foundation was paying the bill, except for the first-class upgrade.

Hours later, someone came by and shook this man until he woke up. The seat was hardly cool when the next crew member fell into the seat. This man was older, with more stripes on his arm. He wiggled around a lot, trying to get comfortable, and I stared out the window into the darkness. He finally fell asleep, but he didn't sleep as soundly as the first man had. I had all this time to study these men, while I was trying not to let them know I was watching. The second man awakened by himself. He stretched and went forward into the cabin. This was a terrible seat to be in. That wicked stewardess hadn't told me that I would have to get used to the whole crew. I might have been next to someone who couldn't sleep either, and then I could have talked or read. I couldn't even have the overhead light on, because these fellows needed to sleep.

The captain came out of the cabin. He had all the stripes on his arm, and his hair was quite gray. My hair was getting gray, too, just trying to make it through this long night.

Captains don't sleep—at least this one didn't. He closed his eyes and rested, but he shifted his position every time there was a slight change in the pitch of the jet engines. I began to listen to the engines, too. He noticed every tiny wobble the airliner made. The pale light of dawn was creeping in from the east. We still had two hours before the flight landed in London. I took one sleeping pill and passed out for half an hour and then was wide awake again.

They managed to get us to London at 0630 hours, just before they would have to feed us breakfast. It didn't matter. I was glad to stand up and get out of that seat.

On the way home from the Indian Ocean, I flew steerage, coach. I was sound asleep in the middle of the afternoon with the window shade pulled down when the captain came on the PA system and said, "Ladies and gentlemen, below is Greenland." He had a deep, melodious voice. I imagined that he was very handsome.

All the shades snapped up, and that was a sight. We were slightly south of the coast. We could see the whole south edge of Greenland—a very rugged coast with bare rock exposed on the hills and the valleys filled with glaciers flowing toward the ocean. Bluish-white icebergs broke off the glaciers and were floating in the blue-green water. It was a scene I shall never forget.

Orly to Madagascar (Africa)

I didn't see a bit of France, just the huge airport at Orly and not much of that. The trip from London to Orly is so short that it was over in a wink.

We did change some dollars for francs, because the next stop after Paris was the French island of La Réunion, in the western Indian Ocean. Air France, which experienced travelers call Air Chance, flies all over Africa, and the flights are really wild.

In 1968, Air France was flying a Boeing 707. That is a huge airplane for the odd little airports in which we landed. The plane from Orly was packed from end to end with a staggering variety of people. There were blacks, Indians, Arabs, Chinese, and a few whites or half-whites. Some passengers were very well dressed, but most looked as scruffy as we did. The stewardesses gave all directions in French, English, and Arabic and occasionally in a Chinese dialect. This took so long that we were well into the air and near the next landing before all the announcements were made.

I saw the boot of Italy just before dark.

The first landing was Cairo, and for some crazy reason, I was prepared to view the pyramids, which might be lighted at night. Instead, we landed in darkness at the end of the tarmac and there was sand all around. No one was allowed off the plane. A Shell oil truck came out of the gloom and refueled the plane. We felt at home seeing the shell on the side of the truck, even though Shell is not an American, but a Dutch-English company.

Why was it so dark here? What a disappointment.

Someone said, "Egypt and Israel are at war." Oh, yes. So the airport was blacked out.

Years later, when I looked at my passport, it was stamped as follows: "This passport is not valid for travel to, in or through The Syrian Arab Republic and the United Arab Republic." The latter included Egypt. After this war, all passports like mine were recalled and the restrictions were stamped over with a friendly message.

I didn't see anything of Egypt except a Shell fuel truck.

Then I gave up the window seat and sat in the middle

seat, hoping to go to sleep. Our chief scientist, Bob Fisher, took the window seat. He pulled the shade down, propped a pillow against the window, put his head on the pillow, and slept for hours. The engineer on my right was resting his eyes.

The Air France stewardesses had all the small babies zipped up in little canvas hammocks, which were attached to slots in the ceiling of the airplane. In flight, the bags swayed gently from side to side. All the babies were quietly sleeping. What a wonderful way to spend the night on that aircraft.

I can't sleep on an airplane and I noticed a lot of others can't either, but the main lights went out and were replaced by small star-shaped patterns on the ceiling. The plane quieted down.

Then we stopped at Djibouti. The terminal was a shed with picnic tables covered with dust, and it was hot in the middle of the night. They had orange pop to sell and postcards with lions resting in the shade under spindly acacia trees. I had a warm orange soda.

The pilots on Air France, at least on this milk run in Africa, are probably ex–jet fighter pilots. They dive straight at the runway, and when they take off, they point the plane at an angle of forty-five degrees and climb—fast.

The babies were still sleeping.

The next stop was Entebbe in Uganda, and we had an hour layover here. People must have been getting on and off, but it seemed as if the stop was just to stretch legs, to refuel, and maybe to change crews. But no one wanted to stay in Uganda. Idi Amin was the president then.

As I walked to the terminal, I saw a lot of soldiers with automatic rifles standing on top the buildings. It makes me nervous to see so many men with guns, but I didn't want to stare or look suspicious. So I strolled from the plane into the terminal. Here it was hot and humid at 0300 hrs. but I didn't realize at that time that the airfield was on the edge of Lake Victoria.

At that time (1968), the airport was an old, pale green building—the building where the Ugandans held the Israelis hostage and from which they were rescued by a SWAT team from Israel. I don't know how the Israelis got underneath that array of soldiers on the roof, but probably the soldiers were only there when they expected a plane to land. Not all that many people want to go to Uganda, in any event.

Food on Air France was terrible. It was jellied ham in many forms—solid, ground up, or in shreds. The butter was okay, from Holland. I ate everything they gave me anyway.

But after Uganda we didn't have anything to drink. They were out of bottled and canned water. They were also out of water for the toilets, and most of the men didn't close the doors into the toilets. In general, women are messier than men, but on this flight, the male passengers took the grand prize. I went to the back galley, just once, to ask for drinking water, and when I saw the plight we were in, I didn't ask again or go to the toilet.

At dawn, we landed at Dar-es-Salaam. The side door of the plane was open, and I could see pale pink clouds and the silhouettes of palm trees through a light rain, a mist. It is sort of fun when you don't know where you are going next. My colleagues were resting.

Air France stewardesses try very hard. This route through Africa must be the way they train the women to be tough. If they survive this mess, then they may get better flights going elsewhere later in their careers.

After this stop, in Tanzania, we had some water and we also had breakfast, which consisted of that gelatinous ham, cheese, and coffee. The aircraft was full of people all of the time.

Then we headed out to sea from East Africa.

The first stop was in Madagascar, at Majunga. The landing strip was short and dusty. The engines roared into reverse to stop the plane, and dust flew up all around us. We careened past a lot of flimsy metal buildings. The brakes were on and the seat belts almost cut us in half. We probably delivered mail here.

The takeoff runway at Majunga was very exciting. It looked like a ski jump, with a long run down and then a short upward ramp to lift the plane out over the ocean. When the jet engines started and we rolled toward the ski jump, the engineer next to me looked at his wristwatch in order to time the event. He didn't think we could get off the runway without falling into the ocean. One second there was paved runway under us, and then with a great rush of speed we soared out over the Indian Ocean.

At each stop through Africa and also here in Madagascar, the stewardesses walked down the aisle and sprayed us with insecticide. That was awful. I guess they were trying to kill insects carrying every sort of disease. They almost killed the passengers.

Madagascar is very intersting to geologists. It is part of Africa that has split away from the continent and is slowly drifting, probably to the north and east. It is believed that the East African Rift Valley, which extends from Tanzania to the Red Sea, will be the next part of the continent to split off and drift away. The rift is marked by grabens, which are huge blocks of the earth's crust that are sinking, and by giant volcanoes. Kilimanjaro is the most famous volcano in the rift zone. But the rift, if it does split away, will take a long time to develop, millions and millions of years, so no one is worrying at the moment, except geologists.

The rivers flowing through Madagascar were a brick red color. These rivers carry the lateritic soils of the island to the blue edge of the Indian Ocean.

When we left Majunga, I tried to get to a bathroom.

"Sit down, madam; we are still climbing," said the stewardess, "and then we will be landing again."

And so we did at Tananareve (now Antananarivo), the capital. Here they had a new airport, with gun turrets on the roof. It looked like a prison. As we walked closer to the buildings, I could see the landscaping, which consisted of a few plants. They had spread chunks of rose quartz under the plantings—sort of the way I would use fir bark at home. All that beautiful rose quartz. I picked up one piece and examined it, then remembered the gun turrets and put it back. Inside the terminal on the underground level was the ladies' rest room. The doors were gone or else they had never put them up. Two soldiers with guns stood guard at where the doors should have been. They could see right into the rest room. Oh, well, other women didn't seem to mind that, so why should I object?

When I went outside again, they were washing our airplane. As we waited for the plane, a complete crew in new blue uniforms, pilots and all, came out of the terminal and climbed the steps into the plane. All the crew members were black.

Right away, I asked, "Are they flying our plane?" Of course I didn't ask an official; I asked our engineer. He didn't know. After all, Africa was the home of the black people.

Then the black crew filed off the plane. We were

astonished. Either Air France was training the people of Madagascar to fly these big planes or this was some sort of ritual. After the black crew filed off, the white crew came out of the buildings and climbed back on the plane. So we flew with the white crew.

The engineer who sat with me all the way from the United States almost never spoke. He also never slept and his eyes looked tired all the time. He sort of disappeared into the darkroom of *Argo* when he finally got on board. I can't remember his name, and I doubt that he remembers me except that he might remember that I said, "What's wrong?" about a thousand times. He was very patient.

La Réunion

Réunion was our first plane stop after Madagascar, and we planned to stay here two days to collect volcanic rocks. It would be a luxury to lie down on a bed after almost twenty-four hours of sitting in a plane or standing around in strange airports.

Réunion is 130 miles southwest of Mauritius near 21° S, 55° E. It is on the edge of the Mascarene Plateau, which is underwater. The plateau was named after a Portuguese navigator, Pedro Mascarenhas, who discovered it in 1513. The more I read, the more I realize that the Portuguese sailed to a lot of places between 1500 and 1600. They managed to move in and integrate with everyone—black, white, brown, or yellow.

The French finally seized the island for themselves,

and the name that stuck is the one derived from "la Réunion des Patriotes," for the French Revolution. The island did not have an indigenous population. Now the people are Creole, blacks, and Indians and other Asians, with a liberal sprinkling of wealthy people from France who follow the sun to this place in the winter.

We all stayed at a small hotel, or rather a large house, something like a tourist home in the eastern United States. The woman manager maintained the typical French colonial tradition of cool aloofness. She was unfriendly.

On the first day, we collected volcanic rocks. If you have to do this in a hurry, then one of the best places is in a dry river channel that comes out of the mountains. We found a good site and collected all the rock types that we could identify with a hand lens—basalts everywhere. We took only fresh samples and tried to find types of different colors that might mean slightly different compositions. Many of the igneous rocks had bright green chunks of olivine (Mg-Fe silicates), which were probably crystal aggregates derived from the floors of the volcanic magma chambers. Everyone has speculated on what a magma chamber looks like underground. I picture it as a cave filled with molten rock that cools now and then between eruptions. That is when crystals settle to the bottom in layers and clots. On the next eruption, the crystals are blown out or float out on lava. We found small volcanic bombs, lava balls about the size of grapefruit with cores of brilliant green crystals of olivine. I collected too many of those. They were very beautiful, but also very heavy. We dragged around several thick cloth sacks and filled these with as much as we could carry. These rocks would go with us by air to Mauritius, then to the ship, and finally to San Diego. So if anyone needs volcanic rocks from Réunion, in the western Indian Ocean, they are at Scripps, stored somewhere. I never seemed to get time to work on them.

Le Volcan (Piton de la Fournaise) is 8,610 feet (2,624 meters) tall and is very active. It last erupted in 1972, several years after we were there, and when we saw the top of the volcano, it looked as if it had erupted just a few years before we arrived. The people said it produced large lava flows. If a volcano produces large flows of lava instead of great eruptions of ash, that tells us a little about what kinds of volcanic rocks are produced in each type. Volcanos that produce a lot of explosions and ash are mountains made of alkali-rich, oxidized basalts, with some andesite. On the other hand, volcanos with fire-fountains and great flows of rapidly moving lava are called tholeiitic basalts, which have smaller amounts of alkali metals, water, and oxygen.

The local lore held that no one could see the top of the volcano because rain clouds shrouded the crest all of the time. Cyclonic storms were frequent during the change in seasons, and this was their springtime.

The second day, we hired a car and driver. I do think the following is true—the smaller the island, the more dangerous the drivers. At least it seemed that way to me. This young man started out at about one hundred kilometers per hour and dodged in and out like a maniac, and as I recall, they drive on the wrong side of the road for me there. I sat in the backseat behind the driver with my eyes closed most of the time.

For no good reason, I would like to die at home or at least in the United States somewhere, not halfway around the world, down under, on the barren flanks of a volcano. The coastal highway had steep cliffs down to the ocean on one side and the high walls of a volcano on the other. Now and then I could peek out and see the same steep cliffs to the ocean and walls of a volcano on the other, but then we turned inland and uphill. Now this jerk had to slow down because the road was all curves and the little Renault didn't have enough power to go uphill fast with four people in it.

I saw an electrical or telephone wire on poles, which started at the bottom of the mountain and went to a little café near the top. On the line, hanging side by side, were thousands of saucer-sized spiders. Were they hanging there to dry out? Were they feeding on flying insects? Did they live there all the time? The driver didn't know and claimed he had never seen them. This was probably his first driving job. I do know that I wouldn't like to have spiders that large in my house.

One of the men in our party became carsick, or perhaps he drank and ate too much the night before. We had to stop a lot to let him erupt. The hotel served excellent French dishes, so I was told, and the guys ate and drank way too much. I dislike French cooking. The goal of the French cook is to cover everything with a sauce so you don't know what you are eating.

The car climbed and climbed, and finally I realized that we were inside a giant volcanic crater. The volcano had exploded and left an enormous amphitheaterlike shell. Now and then the road came close to the interior of the crater walls. The rocks were volcanic breccias, angular fragments of colossal size, welded together into the shield of the volcano. We were in Piton des Neiges (10,069 feet), which the books accurately describe as an "immense, denuded volcano."

Then we did stop to have coffee, which was thick and bitter and expensive—not worth the stop.

After the stop at the café, we went even higher but

I don't know how high. The road was paved with hand-chopped blocks of volcanic rock, and farther up we came to a crew working on the road in the rain. The men were in black slickers. In the rain and mist and the general gloom, they looked like bats. It was spooky.

Our guide stopped and said, "Look over the edge here." I was still dizzy from his driving. The road ended at the edge of a two thousand-foot drop. This is where the volcano had blown up and devoured the road. The landscape was lunar, nothing alive or growing, just all black and deep gray rock, but this couldn't be the moon because it was raining so hard.

We had a much better trip down from the tops of the volcanoes. The driver was getting tired and didn't have to show off for us now. I can't recommend La Reúnion for vacation, but it is a good place to hike upon and inside volcanos among unfriendly people.

Mauritius

When we arrived via air at Mauritius, the research vessel *Argo* was tied up in Port Louis.

Mauritius is about five hundred miles east of Madagascar, near 20° S, 57° E. The main island and the surrounding small islands are volcanic. All of the volcanos are extinct as of now. The coastline is fringed with coral reefs. They mine the coral and process it into cement. An old fort guarding the harbor and many older buildings were built of dark volcanic rock bonded with coral cement.

The Dutch took possession of the island in 1598 and

named it for Prince Maurice of Nassau. The island was originally forested with magnificent stands of mahogany and other hardwoods. All the forests were cut down and the wood shipped out all over the world. The colonists, Dutch, French, and English, introduced rats, pigs, deer to hunt, and most domestic animals.

The French brought black slaves and mosquitoes (*Anopheles*), which carried malaria, from Africa. They think they have conquered malaria on Mauritius, but in the airport at Plaisance, there are posters warning of tuberculosis, malaria, and other diseases. If you read all of the posters, you won't get off there.

Port Louis was a big trade center when the Suez Canal was closed, so the harbor was stuffed with ships and the harbor master kept shuffling them around.

Some of the scientists from the previous leg of the expedition were not ready to get off the ship. This meant that some of us on the upcoming leg had to stay in a hotel until the departing staff left and we could move onto the ship. By now I was very tired and too far from home. I began to worry about going on the ship. What if I was seasick and wouldn't be able to work or even take care of myself? What if I hated the whole expedition? I have a horror of being stuck somewhere I can't leave. That keeps me out of jail. If I got on this ship, I was committed to thirty days. Thirty days is a long time to be on a floating jail.

I talked to the third mate. He was a friendly fellow, and he just happened to be standing at the dock while I was looking at *Argo* and worrying.

"I am afraid to get on the ship," I said.

"Oh, don't be. Look at me. I am afraid to fly on a plane or drive on a freeway. When I get on the ship in San Diego, I have to stay with it for nine months until it gets back to San Diego. Besides, you have come so far. It would be a shame if you didn't go with us," he said.

"Come and see my cabin," he said. "You will like it."

He had a small cabin below the deck and the main stairs came toward his door, so he could see everything if he wanted. The little cabin was filled by his bed. When he closed his door, it would be like a roomette on a train but without the window. Above the bed he had all sorts of shelves with record and tape equipment for music, books, photos of his wife and children, and lamps rigged so he could lie with his head at either end. He had just received a package from his wife—pajamas in a fake leopard skin pattern. Why in the world would a woman send her husband pajamas like that? But he was cheered with his present from home, and he loved his cabin. It looked like a tomb to me. He might as well have been on a submarine. I lied. I told him his cabin was great.

"You will come with us then?"

"Yes, I guess I should. Thank you for talking with me."

Then I went back to the hotel and moped around some more. The hotel was covered with cracked pink stucco and built like a U-shaped fort, probably by the British. I have seen the same design in several British colonies. Since we were twenty degrees south of the equator, the island should have been warm to hot all year round, but it was chilly in September. The building had no heat at all. My bed had an ancient spring and mattress, with sheets and one thin blanket. I was so cold at night that I was stiff and sore all the next day. A tiny Indian man was on duty at night. I asked for more blankets, but he didn't have them. However, he had an electric heater in his room. He turned it on at night so that he would be comfortable.

"Please, you take my electric heater tonight," he said.

"No. What would you do?" He was so small and thin, with not a bit of fat to keep him warm.

"This is what we will do tonight," he said. "You take the heater to keep warm until you fall asleep. When you are asleep, I will quietly come in and take the heater for myself."

The dear man. It worked. I slept all night and I didn't hear him come in to take the heater. He was as quiet as a mouse.

At breakfast in the hotel dining room, all the tables were set but there were only two diners. A man sat at one table reading, and I sat at the opposite end of the room. Why do people do that? The room was silent except for a radio that was broadcasting news from the BBC.

The breakfast menu was short—fruit juice, toast, porridge, and tea or coffee. Okay, I didn't think I liked porridge, but I would try it. The bowl came, heaping full. They give you a lot of porridge. I decided to add some sugar and reached for the sugar bowl. The stuff in it looked like dirty beach sand.

"Please, what is this?"

"It is our sugar from the island, raw sugar."

"Oh, thank you." It was fine, but I had never seen raw sugar. These days raw sugar is about twice the price of white refined sugar. The people here were ahead of us by years.

I moved onto the ship that night. It was warmer than my hotel room, even though it was damp and sitting in the ocean. On board I could have a blanket or two. This must have been a brief cold snap in their spring weather. Everyone said that it was too cold for this time of year. The weather is always abnormal everywhere.

It was better being on the ship. Now I was committed.

On the next day, four of us were asked to eat lunch at the home of a prominent resident, a Mr. Baissac, who met all of the oceanographic vessels. He had welcomed *Argo* and *Horizon* on the last trip here, and he had helped Scripps on the last voyage. After food and new scientific gear were put on board, the captain of *Horizon* had decided on his own that he wanted to leave Port Louis without permission. He got underway but went aground and was apprehended. Scripps was fined $25,000 for this breach of safety. You have to have permission and a pilot boat to lead you out of port. Officials ordered the ship back into port, and the fine grew steadily each day. Mr. Baissac and Dr. Fisher intervened, and somehow Scripps wiggled out of the fine.

On Mauritius, the Baissac family lived in a colonial plantation home built by Alix Baissac's grandfather. Oh, what a lovely home and garden. It was built of stone and wood, a rambling place of mahogany and teak. The doors were ceiling high and made with heavy shutters that could be closed against the hurricanes. The windows were protected in the same fashion.

Baissac was an enthusiastic amateur scientist. He had to show us everything, and he wanted to learn everything we knew. He drove a Renault car, and he took us on whirlwind tours around the big island. We saw cane sugar fields—hundred of acres of sugar planted in amongst boulders and chunks of basalt. Some fields were cleared by simply moving lava rock into long rows. Then the canes were planted in between. Other fields were cleared by expert stone masons who built circular fortlike structures with the excess basalt. The sugar growers had a lot of help from a lot of patient hands, but the political climate was changing. The island workers felt they were being exploited. This was apparent to me, but Baissac didn't seem aware of it yet, or he underestimated the resentment.

Baissac had a big German shepherd, and I recall being surprised that this dog could understand French. Of course, Baissac spoke French at home, but I had never met a dog who could understand French. If I spoke English, the dog just cocked his head and then gave up trying to understand me and walked off. Both the master and the dog were handsome males.

The front of the Baissac home stood at the end of a long curving driveway. The large porch that faced on the gardens was lined with elegant white columns. The Baissacs or more accurately their servants raised vegetables and chickens. We ate their vegetables and I could hear their chickens, but there are so many sounds on tropical islands that chickens just blend right in.

The furnishings inside the Baissac house were from another century. The chairs were floral prints, and there were sofas of teak and mahogany. Some items were a bit worn, but a lot of the furniture had been in this house for at least one hundred years. Chairs at the dining table were covered with petit point fabric, obviously embroidered by the Baissac women. The draperies were heavy patterned brocade. The floor was built of planks of mahogany with scattered hooked and braided rugs. It was all so lovely. I wish now that I had stared openly at everything or taken notes. This house exuded a quiet elegance, yet it was cozy, too. The Baissacs made the home seem cozy.

Baissac's wife, Alix, and her mother ran the house. I remember her mother well. She retained the dress of the last century, and it was charming. Once I saw two old women, sisters probably, dining at the old Marcus Daly Hotel in Anaconda, Montana. They were also dressed like this. I know that you can observe all of this in films and on "Masterpiece Theater," but sitting across from these authentic elders in their antique clothes is quite an experience. I don't know about the minds of the ladies in Montana, but this elderly French lady had a very sharp, clear mind.

I asked Madame Baissac if I could use her bathroom.

"Certainly. Come with me and we will go into my private salon."

The bathroom was large and had a water closet with the tank of wood attached to the wall above. These fittings are coming into style again, but the one in her room was very old, made of mahogany, and carved with birds and flowers.

Then we sat down at the table to eat lunch. I always think of lunch as a small meal, a sandwich or soup, but each place setting had several forks and spoons. Does one work from the outside in? Why didn't I ask something like, "Are we having lots of courses?" No, that is gauche. I decided to watch what the others did, but the servant started with me. As usual, I took too much, cauliflower in a cheese sauce—very delicious, but filling. Then I had a big salad of garden vegetables. Finally we had chicken breasts rolled around something—I think it was a small squid with cheese—and a fruit tart, which was filled with ripe pineapple. There was a lot of wine, too, but they didn't push it.

Mrs. Baissac's mother went to her room for a nap. The rest of us sat on the veranda in rocking chairs. Ah, this is the life!

But there was a car parked in the driveway, not at the entrance to the main house, but back away and off to the side so as not to be obtrusive. Jean Baissac paid no attention to the car or the four dark-skinned men in it. On the other hand, his wife, Alix, was very upset that Baissac ignored the car. I could gather, from what little French I know, that she wanted Baissac to talk to the men.

Baissac finally strolled out to talk to the men. It was not friendly chatter. When he came back to the porch, Baissac said that the men were labor leaders organizing the island workers. The workers came from the sugar fields and mills. They wanted more money, less work, and some land of their own. I must admit that Baissac treated them like dirt.

Dr. Fisher was in Mauritius about ten years later and I asked him, "How are the Baissacs? Did you see them?"

"Yes," he said. "It is very sad. Of course, Mrs. Baissac's mother is dead, and he and his wife had to move out of the big house. Now they live in a tiny home that used to house the servants."

The main house is now owned by a wealthy Indian merchant.

After this delicious lunch and the small talk and sitting on the veranda, we had to go back to Port Louis, to the ship. What a letdown. The port was filled with sick-looking people, amputees sitting around on the cobblestones begging, and lots of starving dogs with tumors on their bodies. Most people don't "see" these horrors or are able to ignore them. I see too much and wish that I could clean the place, help the sick, get the dogs off the streets, and on and on. But there is no solution. This place is a tiny dot of land with enormous numbers of people and animals. The island paradise has turned into a black hole.

A Party

The research vessel *Argo* came from Sri Lanka (Ceylon, then) west across the Indian Ocean to Port Louis, Mauritius.

The main exports from Mauritius are sugar and tea. Ships in the harbor were loaded with bags of sugar stored on the decks. The bags were tightly woven burlap, but since it rained all of the time, I couldn't figure out why the sugar didn't dissolve. Probably the top bags melted and sealed the ones below. I would think that sugar would be a sticky, slippery cargo.

Sometimes *Argo* was tied up at dockside, but other times we had to walk across other ships to get to ours. One ship that we had to cross was a small, greasy thing. We had to crawl over it and climb a ladder to get on board our ship. There were times when ships were tied up three-deep. We had a Japanese fishing ship attached to us, and I could watch the crew from my cabin. They had a lot of shark mouths hanging on the wheelhouse, and the men slept on deck in colorful bags with an awning over them. They scrubbed the wood deck every day and seemed to enjoy the work.

Most of our scientists, the ones on board from Sri Lanka to Mauritius, left the ship and flew home to San Diego. Part of the the crew rotated here, and a new captain came on board. It is cheaper to rotate crew and scientists than to move the ship.

The captain and the new scientist in charge decided to have an open-ship party for the locals who were interested in research vessels or who would like to come to a party. This was good PR. In 1968, the super spy ship

USS *Pueblo* was operating as an "oceanographic research vessel." The ship was seized by North Korea. That deception hurt all oceanographic institutions for years.

We could show them that we were not a spy ship although the U.S. Navy supported the research. Our navy wanted the maps of the topography of the ocean floor—naturally. The United States Navy wants to know where to hide their submarines, and so do the Russians. I hope they bump into each other.

A partial list of guests was drawn up by the U.S. Consulate in Madagascar and sent to the ship. Then we could add to the list as we wished. I had nothing to do with the planning, but I heard them talking. Cases and cases of vodka and gin and lots of Scotch whiskey, Johnny Walker Red Label, were hoisted on deck.

The crew had scraped and sanded our deck, and we even had a thin paint job. We had to get the deck dry before the guests arrived. I tried to rearrange my cabin in order to make it look presentable in case someone looked in. We had thin gray-white bedspreads, and I turned mine over and made the bed especially carefully. But what can you do with a cell? Our ship was moved to dockside for the party. Ever since then, I can remember which side is port or starboard. Port is on the left as one faces forward.

Lots of tables were set up on deck, with white linen cloths and glasses, ice, alcohol, mixers, and hundreds of delicate little sandwiches. This party must have been catered, because we couldn't possibly find all these goodies in our galley. It was a beautiful evening with a gentle breeze and fluffy strawberry clouds over the mountains. We were elegant.

The scientific crew was to take groups of people down from the main deck into the laboratory and explain what we were doing. Since I didn't know what we were doing, they asked me to stand at the gangplank and welcome people aboard. Even that little task made me nervous, so I decided to say, "Welcome," and just point the way to the next group going into the laboratory.

The chief scientist said to me, "Keep the crew off the women."

"What?"

"Keep the crew off the women guests."

"What do you mean by that?"

He explained, "The crew members and some staff members join the party and they get drunk and then they make passes at the departing women." Gawd, how could we be elegant? I didn't believe him really, until later.

I don't remember a lot about how the male guests were dressed. Some were in tuxedos or simple white suits, one with a red sash, but most of the women were dressed in Paris designs. The list our embassy supplied did not include your man-on-the-street types.

Of course, the Indian women with the colorful saris always look beautiful and graceful. Part of the fabric flows out behind. I don't know how they got up and down vertical stairs into the laboratory, but probably like gliding birds. And their hair, either braided in elaborate fashion or flowing about their shoulders, was black and glistening. They wore a lot of gold bracelets on arms and ankles.

Then there was a young Frenchwoman wearing a white sheath dress with plunging neckline and a rose pinned at the V. She was so classy with white satin high-heeled shoes. White on a ship like this—although we were very cleaned up for the party, still there was grease everywhere. An oriental woman came on board, unescorted. She wore a long pale yellow gown with slits up each side to the knee. Part of the fabric was hand-painted with tiny flowers and birds. Her skin was a pale porcelain peach color, and she wore long white gloves. She was absolutely lovely, and I made a mental note to see that she got off the ship safely.

In the meantime, I felt like the country cousin. I did have one dress along, but it was serviceable and plain. I think I had to wear my tennis shoes. No, I had new slippers. I bought them in Mauritius, and I remember trying them on in an Indian shop. When I pulled on the right slipper, it had a straight pin stuck in the sole and it stuck me in the foot. I had to have a tetanus shot.

I was dressed well enough to be the official greeter, and I was glad to be on deck.

As the bottles opened and drinks were served, the ship's crew descended on the drinks and food. It must have been part of their fringe benefits, being allowed to eat and drink everything in sight. Further, most of them got drunk very fast, probably from trying to drink up everything instantly.

Soon several crew members were standing with me. Some of the guests were departing, and—yes—the guys try to squeeze and kiss the women and others tried to pat the pretty bottoms. I needed another pair of arms to shield the women as they left the ship. It didn't matter in the least that I tried to stare down these amorous guys, and I even yelled at them between the groups of departing guests. How come the male guests didn't beat our crewmen for grabbing at their women?

How could you have a party with these clowns trying to ruin it? The whole ship was crazy. But most of the women, going along with the festive atmosphere, didn't seem to mind too much.

With my duties as official greeter and all this commotion at the gangplank, I didn't get a sandwich or a drink.

Dining at Sea

At Port Louis, Mauritius, some people who came to the ship's party came back the next day to watch *Argo* leave for the next leg of the expedition—which usually would last twenty-nine days. They stood on the dock and waved, and we waved back from the ship.

One of the mates came by and muttered, "I wouldn't wave yet if I were you."

"Oh, why?"

"The tide is out and we are loaded with fuel and water. We may be stuck in the mud," he said.

"Don't you know if we are stuck?"

The engines were on—I could feel that—but the captain had not ordered us to move. My arm went limp, and I went back to sit on my bunk. Stuck in the mud, we could be here for hours, days, waving.

But the ship groaned a bit, then moved, and we pulled away from the dock. The mate came running in yelling we are okay. Do they try to fool me all the time, or was it for real?

So we sailed from Port Louis, Mauritius, and we could look back to see the mountains (volcanoes). A light rain was falling in the sunshine. Some of the volcanoes were weathered into sharp crags and other exotic shapes. The colors there were brilliant. There were all the possible shades of green from pale yellow-green to deep blue-green. The bare volcanoes were pink, mauve, purple, and blue. We watched big double rainbows form and fade. For the moment, I thought, this was like being on an elegant cruise ship. You couldn't find better scenery or a more exotic island anywhere on earth.

The ship was flying all sorts of flags—farewell, we love you, be back soon, USA, Mauritius—lots of flags, but we were still in the stream, not in the open ocean.

When we did hit the Indian Ocean, it was like falling into a giant earthquake that did not stop after a few minutes, and the aftershocks were as bad or worse than the main event. *Argo* was such a little thing in those waves. It didn't help to have the old sailors say, "Oh, we were in a smaller ship in a typhoon and the ship started to break up," or, "This is just a little rough."

I did see two United States cruisers in Port Louis. Some of the officers told me what to expect.

"We can't stand up on the deck unless we hang onto ropes," they said.

Of course, cruisers are narrower than the old, broad *Argo* and they would roll and pitch a lot more than we did. I was most worried about falling down and breaking a leg. A broken arm would be okay, but a leg—if you couldn't get around, this group on *Argo* might stuff your legs into concrete and throw you overboard. They didn't plan to miss a minute of ship time. Everyone was worrying about "ship time, ship time." It is very expensive. Probably astronomers fight around about telescope time or physicists for accelerator time. Everything in science that depends on some sort of vehicle or big apparatus is costly to keep running and takes many sharp engineers and technicians working twenty-four hours a day.

It is cheaper to be a geologist, on land, with just a pack on your back and a pick in your hand and lunch in a paper sack.

My roommate, Barbara, a graduate student in oceanography, was the first casualty. She just stayed in her bed and slept. Or she tried to sleep. She was smart to stay horizontal.

Our chief scientist sent me to find Professor John, our dear colleague from England. I found him sitting on the floor in the corner of his darkened cabin with his head on his knees. The scene reminded me of horror photos of patients in a mental institution.

"John, what is wrong?"

He just whispered that he was very seasick. I made him lie down on the floor, put a pillow under his head, and told him to stay there—that I would be right back. We hadn't been at sea for more than an hour. Over the next several days, John became worse and worse. He had vertigo, too. He couldn't eat and he couldn't stand up. Members of the crew moved him to a cabin below deck where it was dark and there was less motion. He just couldn't get better. Later he admitted that he was always sick at sea, but each time he hoped he would be okay. Why would a guy punish himself like that?

Then I remembered a little home remedy that the pediatrician had told me about when our children were small. If they were vomiting for a while, he told me to give them some Coke or 7-Up. The bubbles help and the sugar acts like an IV and they don't become dehydrated. Fortunately, we had a cold drink machine on board and we collected a lot of quarters for John and he survived on 7-Up. John should have made a commercial for the soft drink industry. Sailors are not sympathetic with people who are seasick.

During the first two weeks at sea, John lost about twenty pounds and was very pale. We were southwest of the island of Diego Garcia where the British had an air base. There was some discussion about going in there and handing John over to his countrymen, but I don't think that John wanted to go in there, not the way he looked. Besides, it was several days out of the way and we would lose ship time. P.S.: Now we have Diego Garcia and it is a U.S. air base.

I ate a lot. The one cook was a good pastry chef. There were lots of goodies at breakfast (0700). Then too, food is out all the time on a research vessel, so you can snack continuously. I found cans of delicious Australian fruit, salad-sized chunks of good, ripe fruit. I hid some cans in my bunk. Soon I could not fit in my jeans and they were starting to fall apart and wear thin in the washing machine. In fact, I got so scared about having nothing to wear that I looked at the new cotton towels that came on board at Sri Lanka. Perhaps I could make a simple dress by hand-sewing the shoulders and sides of the towels into a sheath. First I selected two bath towels with green borders and washed them and dried them in the drier in the ship's stack. After the drying, they were about the size of tea towels. There were no new clothes on this trip. I checked the sheets, but they were thin and worn. Besides, how do you wear a sheet unless you have grown up in India?

Lunch came too early, at 1100 hours. The crew managed to get into the dining room first. One day we had clam chowder, with big clams, and it looked delicious from a distance. But the men ahead dug out the clams and there was just broth and potatoes left.

They teased each other. "Hey, those clams have to swim." They had all the clams heaped into bowls without the liquid, or at least not much of it.

Barbara started eating and not sleeping so much. And she exercised in our cabin by hanging onto the sink and swinging her legs out like a dancer. I retreated to the lower bunk.

The cooks put rubber netting on the tables to keep the utensils from crashing to the floor. Before they did that, I never took a knife because I was afraid of stabbing the next diner as the ship rolled. Our dear friend John got thinner and thinner, but he was able to come out on deck and sit a bit, always with a can of 7-Up in hand. There were only two deck chairs on *Argo*. You had to keep working; you couldn't just sit. The chairs were thin aluminum tubing with a plastic webbing—not much to hold onto. You had to sit in them to keep them from flying off the ship.

Perhaps our most worrisome time was when the head chef got drunk and fell in a gangway. He hurt his back, and they put him into sick bay for a few days. We had some carrots with the wilted greens still attached. We made a bouquet of carrot greens to help speed his recovery. One night we made some popcorn in the galley. I know that I put everything back in its place, but the chefs made a giant protest. No one was allowed in the galley except the cooks. This commotion went all the way up to the captain, and he ruled, no more popcorn. How come they had popcorn on the ship if we couldn't eat it?

The only time I felt slightly ill was one day in the wheelhouse. The second mate asked me just to watch the horizon while he went to get coffee. They had to watch all the time for other ships, even though we were not in shipping lanes. Perhaps we were also watching for the men overboard from other ships. I found that I could crash around in a rough sea and even enjoyed hanging in the stairwells to get that weightless feeling as the ship pitched, but I could not watch the horizon—at least not for a long time or I would have been sick.

Our captain drank too much. This was a "dry" ship, but I saw crates and crates of scotch and a lot of gin. The crew covered for the captain, but near the end of the voyage, he didn't come to the dining room at all. Probably he couldn't stand the thought of one more expedition.

Two brown albatrosses followed the ship for the last ten days of the voyage. Who knows where they came from, but they carefully checked out the garbage that the cooks dumped into the ocean. I didn't see them rest on the rigging. They were gliding all the time. However, they did rest on the water while eating.

A crewman asked me to help in the freezer room. It was a big room, and a lot of the crates were broken and the food was sliding around on the floor. That day he was trying to catch big grayish pink chunks of corned beef. They just looked dreadful. How could we eat that stuff—that color? We did get the meat back into crates and lashed to the hull. The meat looked like water buffalo from India, or maybe it was seven months old from San Diego.

I won't eat corned beef ever again.

Twenty-four Hours

An oceanographic vessel works twenty-four hours a day. For some reason, I thought we would anchor at night and go to sleep. Well, you can't anchor in most of the world oceans because they are too deep and costs are astronomical, so the scientific crew rotates around the clock, four hours on the instruments and then the next rotation for four hours. I hated that schedule because all I wanted were the rocks that we hoped to dredge off the bottom in deep fracture zones and on ridge tops. I didn't care that much if we knew their precise location and depth. Our chief scientist knew where we were most of the time.

Of course, you can't goof off on a ship at sea that costs five thousand to ten thousand dollars a day to operate. Since 1968, costs have risen sharply. But even the astronauts go to sleep on space voyages. Houston turns off the communication system, and the people sleep. Not so on the research vessel *Argo*.

The major work at sea included the continuous recordings of depth and, on our leg of the expedition, dredge hauls for rock whenever we arrived at the right places, day or night. A successful dredge haul usually takes eight to twelve hours, sometimes longer. You can't see the ocean floor unless you lower a huge, costly camera, and you can't have the camera and dredge out at the same time. When the rock dredge is out on a heavy, long cable, you can't see what it is scraping over or what is coming up in the heavy chain bag until you have it on the deck. However, it is much more fun to dredge for rocks in the daylight. This is geologic fishing at its best.

On the sixth night out, after two unsuccessful dredge hauls, I went screaming out on deck and into the laboratory, yelling about how terrible it was to be floundering in a heavy sea with the cable out six thousand meters or whatever. Barbara and I couldn't sleep; we could barely stay in our bunks with the ship rolling so hard. If the dredge gets hung up on the bottom and they are afraid to pull too hard for fear of breaking the cable, then the stern of the ship is pulled down into the water and waves are pounding the deck. Seawater comes over the coamings into the laboratory. Oh, men make such a mess.

Later, we heard that the Russian ship *Vityaz,* at a similar station north of us, almost had a mutiny because the biologists didn't want to be hung up for days by geologists at the same dredging position. Fortunately, on this expedition we didn't try to combine geologists and biologists.

When we were dredging, and I guess it was the same on the Russian research vessel, the ship was just barely holding its own in the heavy seas at perhaps two or three knots. The ship was wallowing like a wounded sea monster. When we were not dredging, we tried to maintain nine knots, and that is a lot more comfortable. Well, I did make an ass of myself, but not too many people heard me. It did some good, though. One of the mates came up with two guardrails to put on our bunks, so we wouldn't fall out of the damned things.

When I first saw our research ship, *Argo,* in Mauritius, I was appalled. It was a United States Navy rescue and salvage tug built in 1944. It was 213 feet long and forty feet wide and had a "cruising speed of thirteen knots." Perhaps when it was new it could cruise along at that speed, but not when I was aboard. *Argo* had a huge hoist on the starboard. This hoist gave the ship a permanent list of about four degrees. Nothing was level anywhere. *Argo* had something like 900,000 hours on it, or about 160 times around the Earth. Those numbers are not correct, so don't try to calculate with them, but the ship was old and worn out. It was gracious of the U.S. Navy to send us out in this old tub. If the navy had not given *Argo* to Scripps, they would have had to sink it to get rid of it.

One day I was out on the stern rolling some big rocks around when the ship turned so quickly and sharply that the ship swept the waves smooth. I wondered, *What the hell is he doing now?* I thought the chief scientist had changed course suddenly. It seemed as if we turned too fast, but I worked on deck for a little while trying to get the rocks from the last dredge haul separated into various rock types.

When I went into the lab, it was empty. No one on duty at all? A crewman came by. "They're all in the galley," he said.

The rudder had broken. The big chains that steer the rudder broke loose from the hull. *This never happens.* The next thing I found out was that they were cutting a hole in the galley floor with an acetylene torch. This was the only way they could get to the chains that operated the rudder. The chief engineer told us to stand back because they were using the torch right above the fuel tanks. Which lifeboat was I supposed to get into? Did I have a life jacket?

I get angry at the U.S. Navy all over when I think that here we were in the Indian Ocean and couldn't steer. This crummy tub was a derelict. Fortunately, the weather was not as rough as usual and the ocean was fairly calm. I don't know if *Argo* sent out a distress call, but they did warn other ships, if there were any near, to stay out of the area because we were out of control. We did have marvelous engineers and welders. Also, we were fairly close to Mauritius. The work crew patched the huge chain and put the floor back in the galley. We could steer now, but they wanted to get into port as soon as possible. Me, too.

The cabin for the two women was six by nine feet, with two bunks, a four-drawer chest bolted to the wall, and a washbasin, which was a luxury. It also had a porthole and a door onto the deck. We could open the porthole, but the door was closed when we were at sea or we would have drowned in our bunks. Our tiny cell entered on what was called the lounge. Other cabins entered on the lounge, too—one for the captain, with its own bathroom, and another for the chief scientist, which was similarly equipped. The women had to go down the gangway to find the head and shower. I am complaining because at Scripps the men called these expeditions cruises and this is not what I regard as a cruise ship.

I arrived before Barbara, so I asked for a bucket and some bleach and soap and washed the green and reddish streaks of mildew and crud off the walls. Then I attacked the floor, but that was all corroded. It looked and was dirty all of the time. I hated to step on our floor in my bare feet. I put my stuff in the lower bunk and made up the bed. When Barbara came on board, she was miffed because I had the bottom bunk.

"Look here," I said. "I am old enough to be your mother, and you wouldn't put your mother up there."

She threw her things on the upper bunk. Then we got to the chest of drawers. She would have it her way here. We each had every other drawer, with Barbara in the top drawer. Oh, we did have a small closet. With all the fixed bunks, chest, closet, and sink, we didn't have much room to get around on the floor.

I had to promise Barbara that I would keep my sheet off the edge of the bottom bunk so if she had to go to the head at night, she wouldn't slip on my sheet and fall to the floor. It was warm to hot most of the time, so we didn't have blankets.

As I said, Barbara was a graduate student in oceanography, but she didn't want to be at sea. She thought she was a theoretician and hadn't planned to get into this messy, greasy work. She would not work on the depth recorder. Someone assigned her to work on the computer. She finally produced a computer outline of *Argo,* made with little x's. Everyone applauded.

I said that I would work on all the dredge hauls and also monitor the depth recorders when the regular scientists wanted to see a movie on Sunday night. I also did all the laundry for the scientific crew. Now that sounds easy, but it was not. The washing machine on *Argo* was below deck in the bow. The washer was the old wringer type with two rinsing tubs, all of which were bolted to the floor (deck). I first washed Barbara's and my clothes in the clean water and then washed the clothes of the men in our rinse water. The men had more oil and dirt on their clothes. Besides—women and children first.

When the ship was pitching, the water in the tubs rose up and fell back into the machine. It was exciting to watch. The drier was in the stack on the main deck. I ran back and forth a lot. Coming down the gangway, one day, with a load of dirty clothes in my arms, I realized a nude man was coming toward me. The only thing he had on was a towel over his arm. It was just one glance, then I walked ahead looking at the floor and he passed me.

One day I was down under washing and the metal of the hull was creaking and groaning. I wondered if this old ship would fall apart. Someone yelled, "Dammit, I am going to slow this ship before it falls apart, and I don't care what anyone says." Then we slowed fast. The water rose on the last pitch and then slurped out all over the floor. Our captain complained that I washed too much and the ship would run out of water. More complaints—I was too clean.

It was the third mate who slowed *Argo* that day, and he was right.

I should note here that the ship's crew and the scientific crew were separated. The ship's crew was governed by the captain, and the scientific crew fought around among themselves, but the chief scientist made all the decisions. Of course, if the captain felt the scientists were getting the ship into a dangerous situation, then the captain could overrule the scientists.

After *Argo* returned to San Diego, the U.S. Navy reclaimed it and it was mothballed. Finally, someone from the Far East bought it and planned to tow it across the Pacific Ocean. Near Hawaii, the new owner "lost" the ship. *Argo* was found adrift with no one on board. I wonder if the washing machine was on board.

Depth Recording at Sea

The weather was horrid. It was dominated by continuous anticyclones. According to reports from other ships, there were nineteen men overboard and missing in the western Indian Ocean. I was certain they were all drowned or eaten. The sky was cloudy most of the time, and the navigators had a fit because they could not get good star or sun positions. We had a satellite computer on board, but the system was new and not working well. In fact, it was so bad that the programmer built in a rating system for the satellite numbers for latitude and longitude. Most locations were rated "very poor."

The chief scientist was crabby. He wanted to know where we were on his maps in order to locate dredge hauls of rocks we hoped to collect. Also, he was trying to upgrade his topographic and geophysical maps.

The first time that I was on the depth recorder, the ship was rolling hard and my biggest problem was to keep hold of my yellow pencil. After hours of fighting around for it on the lab bench, I held it in my mouth. It was sometimes even difficult to remember where my mouth was. I was not seasick, but there was an awful lethargy that I call motion dullness.

For me, this motion dullness was so bad that I had to think how to get dressed. Take off the pajamas, fold them, then put on the clothes from the top of the pile down. Yes, first the underclothes, then the jeans, then the shirt. Sometimes, I had the shoes on first and then couldn't get the jeans over them. Then you should tie your shoelaces. Most people wore go-aheads or whatever those sandals are called. I would have broken a leg in them. As the ship rolls, you tend to step or fall out of the sandals. On the other hand, I had tennis shoes called boaters and, yes, they are for boats. People shuffle a bit when they walk. You can't shuffle in a boater. The shoes hang on tight. You make a few tiny steps and then a big awkward leap to catch the ship as the deck rolls toward or away from you.

I became better at most of this after the first week. I started to liven up a bit, and I became crabby, too. I was still fighting to hang onto my pencil and the laboratory notebook.

The research vessel *Argo* had the laboratory below deck in a dull gray room. See how the dullness starts? The ship was all gray. The person in charge of the lab had to make notations every ten minutes on the depth to the bottom of the ocean floor. Later, others could make contour and geologic maps from these data. We had to try to get good numbers for the depth to the ocean floor beneath the ship. But we didn't have good locations because the celestial navigation was poor and checking of locations via satellite still in its infancy on this ship. One night I looked at the map of our location and when the sun came out the next morning, we were about four inches farther along on the course than the night before. That was a *big* change involving a hundred miles or more, perhaps a lot more. I didn't ask what happened. Somebody was bound to become angry at me. Everyone was crabby about the weather.

I was on my second watch and didn't know exactly how well I was doing. There was a twenty-four-hour clock on the wall to my left that was set at Greenwich mean time. I got all mixed up by this time business. We were supposed to eat breakfast at 0700 local time and keep notations in Greenwich time. And the work was dull. In front of me was a graph with a needle marking the depth. It was set at a scale to magnify the topography by ten to one hundred times, or whatever, depending on the topography of the ocean floor.

Off to my right was another scale and pen with the vertical scale set much smaller; maybe that pen was set to scale. That pen was marking an almost straight line, with just a few gentle valleys and or ridges. It was essentially flat. But no one instructed me to watch both graphs. In fact, I didn't see the second graph until much later. I know what to do now, years later, because I have thought about it a lot since then.

I was on the second watch and doing fine, with pencil in mouth and recording book on my lap, when the needle in front of me started to rise almost straight up and slid along the top of the paper—flat. Even I knew that I should change scale, but how?

Then I started to yell, "help," but I shut up. The transponders on the hull were pinging away in a different tone, shallower and faster, but no one showed me how to change scale and when I get excited and am missing something important, I just give up. No one came running to help so I just sat there, numb. A crabby lab tech finally walked by, and I signaled frantically.

"Oh, its okay," he said. "This part of the Indian Ocean is well known. They put you on this watch to see if you can figure things out. We just went over a big seamount."

I should have gone to the chief scientist and chewed him out. I hate to make huge mistakes. But I didn't say anything. Our chief scientist thought that if I could analyze a rock, I should know what to do on a ship. I had never been on a ship.

Then we passed over that mountain on the sea floor and the needle came down into the range of, say, four thousand meters, and it was flat there for quite a while. On the other scale, the one to the right, was a little thing that looked like a pimple on the ocean floor. That was the seamount that I had missed, and it was drawn to scale.

The chief scientist came by and stood behind me watching. That made me nervous. The recording paper was blocked off in units of ten.

Fisher said, "What is the reading now?"

I said something like "4,130-odd meters."

He said, "What do you do in between tens?"

There was a long silence while I searched my ocean-dullness-fogged brain for the word *interpolate*.

I said, "Yes, 4,136 meters."

He said, "Four thousand, one hundred and thirty-seven meters."

Okay, at this stage in my life I was used to having men correct me. It was his program anyway. Besides at four thousand meters deep, I was not certain how close these readings could be in any event. But if they could dredge some rocks off the bottom, I could take them home to my laboratory and study them in peace and quiet.

I did most of my thinking in the shower. When the sound wave sent to the bottom returns as a quiet spaced ping, we were in deep water. When the sound changed to that fast, sharp ping, we were getting shallow in a hurry and I had to change scale to keep the needle on the graph paper. I would try to be ready next time.

Taking a shower on a rolling or pitching ship is dangerous. The shower was another gray cubicle, with pipes running all around near the ceiling and not so near the ceiling. It was a death trap. Thirteen hundred hours was a good time to take a shower. Lunch was over and the shifts were changed. This is also siesta time, if one is not assigned to some duty and there is no one around wanting to get into the shower. Now, this is tricky, also because the shower room is very small, maybe three feet by three feet, with a soap dish on the wall. You have to get in there, then undress, reach around outside the door, and hang your clothes on a hook outside. You had to remember to get your soap and shampoo inside. Otherwise some jerk always took the soap away.

Now I was inside, and the only way to stand up and not get bruised all over was to press my rear hard against the wall and sort of hunch over. This works okay even in wild seas. Except one day when it was fairly calm, I got all soaped up and then this terrible shrieking siren started howling right beyond the shower door. I think I saw the red color of the bell and the word FIRE, but I didn't pay attention to it.

Instantly, you know there is a fire, and the sound is enormous in the tiny passageway and shower. The water turned off in the shower. I was exhausted anyway, and I thought, *just go down with the ship, because you can't get into a lifeboat when you are covered with soap and have no clothes on.* But the will to live takes over, and I quickly wiped off some of the soap and grabbed my clothes and put them on. Maybe I could swim for a while and they would pick me up. The water was quite warm, and I worried about sharks. I could do a lot of worrying in a hurry.

When I did get on deck, there they all were in their life preservers scowling at me. "It is a drill," they said. Most of them knew it was a drill. The ship had two big lifeboats. The captain mans one lifeboat and the chief scientist the other. I guess we could all squeeze into those boats. After they stopped fussing at me, I was assigned to the captain's lifeboat.

Now I was really disgruntled. There must be a bulletin board on this vessel, and I had better find it. Maybe I could learn what was going to happen next.

Dredging

Of course, I worked with volcanic rocks dredged from the ocean bottom and I heard staff members talk about how to dredge for rocks, but you do have to see it for yourself to realize how difficult the chore. You need a lot of maps of the underwater topography, and it is imperative that the chief scientist knows what he is doing. Bob Fisher had made the maps and he could dredge. Some of it is luck, but most is skill and perseverance. When I would give up, Fisher would persevere.

I used to sit outside at lunch at Scripps and hear them talk about the CABLE. It had to be long and strong, and it had to wind up and wind off a huge drum. Still, I couldn't visualize the operation until I was on the ship.

They had a large A-frame mounted on the stern, and the cable ran over a wheel in it to a rock dredge weighing from five hundred to a thousand pounds. The dredge consisted of a rectangular iron frame, with teeth at the edge meant to break off and scoop up rocks. Attached to the iron frame was a huge chain bag. The idea is to drag the dredge into cracks of submarine rocks, and break them off. The rocks roll back into the chain bag behind, sort of like catching a fish in a landing net, if you are lucky.

The two best dredging sites are at the crests of the oceanic ridges where the seafloor is separating and in and near the cross fractures, which are deep valleys along fault zones that cut the major ridges roughly at right angles to the ridge crests.

The first two dredge hauls came up empty. It is so suspenseful and nerve-racking not to know for sure if anything is in the dredge until it comes into sight. By chance, I guess, we came to many dredge sites in the middle of the night. You could bet we would be in position to lower the dredge near midnight, give or take an hour.

After the first week of bitching, mostly to myself and Barbara, about the dreadful weather, I did settle down and try to help. Everyone was inside the labs when the dredge was out. One person had to sit at the PDR (precision depth recorder) and call out the depths to the ocean floor minute by minute, and the others were watching the tensiometer. That is a gauge that records how many pounds of strain the dredge is exerting on the cable. There was a red zone on the tensiometer, which meant an amount of great strain, so you should back off and stop pulling or you could break the cable and lose the dredge and possibly the cable, too. We were in constant discussions via intercom with the bridge so they could synchronize our speed with the tension on the cable. I think we had a backup cable, or part of a cable, that could be spliced onto the cable in use if part broke off.

I remember one dredging station just because it was so early in the morning, about 0200 hours, and I was reading off the depths. We were drifting slowly, so the depths didn't change a lot. I decided to change my voice into that of a telephone operator who enunciates carefully. "Seven thousand, eight hundred, fifty-two meters." I could have said, "7852." (Now, of course, we don't get an operator who enunciates slowly and clearly on the telephone, now we get a recording.) Everyone was tired and worn out, so you have to put a bit of humor into an operation at 2:00 A.M.

When the dredge came into sight, it was full to the top with rocks. They were dumped on the deck. Some chunks were the size of boulders—not round, but angular. Many different rock types were in this dredge haul. I could see that in the pale light of dawn. There were no basalts, which were common on the ridge crests. These rocks were much heavier, full of Fe-Mg silicates, called ultramafic rocks (dunite, pyroxenite, and lherzolite, some altered to serpentinites), and coarsely crystalline olivine and two-pyroxene gabbros. All of the rocks were very different from anything anyone had seen from the oceans.

These rocks we dredged came from a deep segment of a fracture zone in the oceanic crust. Fisher always hoped that he had broken off fresh rocks from bedrock. I thought they came from rockslides. It didn't matter at all, because the rocks we had told an amazing story.

The sea was very rough, so I pushed and shoved the larger pieces closer to the center of the deck. I didn't want anything to wash overboard. Then everyone fell into bed. I didn't even go back to look the next day.

The second day after this last haul of rocks, even Professor John felt well enough to go out and look. We had heavy ultramafic rocks, full of magnesium silicate minerals. They were somewhat similar to the composition and mineralogy of stony meteorites. And there were Ti-Fe gabbros, many types of gabbro, anorthosite, which contained calcium-rich plagioclase, and some rocks with tiny dikelets of granitic rock. On land, if someone laid out all of these rocks for me, I would say they were from a stratified igneous complex. Apparently, the lower crust of the ocean had been invaded by intrusions of mafic basaltic magma, which had cooled slowly and formed rock layers of different compositions—probably with the heavy minerals at the bottom, then with lighter minerals such as plagioclase near the top, and finally with tiny dikelets of the last liquid of granitic composition. The dikelets were about two centimeters thick and were sodium-rich granite instead of potassium-rich granite, which is common on the continents.

The Russians, to the north of us, dredged "chromitite," which I assume was a rock rich in chromite, a very heavy mineral. Most chromium ores come from stratiform sheets, as in Africa and the Soviet Union.

Another dredge haul from the crest of the Central Indian Ridge was full of shiny black basalts. All of the basalts had a chilled, glassy surface. Many samples contained two or three thin layers of glassy flow superimposed one upon the other. The lava was extremely fluid even at great depth in cold water. And we had cavernous pieces of basalt from which the still fluid cores spilled out into the ocean. Where the lavas were extruded through abyssal muds, the rocks were chilled into exotic curled, rolled, folded, and bulbous forms. Some samples of basalt recovered from the ridge crest had fragments of red mud baked onto and partially engulfed by lava. These basalts were fresh and very young. I could see the petrographic and chemical work stacking up for years to come.

My favorite pieces of basalt were "eggs"—about the size of a chicken egg, but shiny and black. And there were some very tiny eggs about the size of the end of a little finger. *I have to get some of these basaltic jewels to set in a pin or a necklace,* I thought, but they all went into the scientific collections.

There were rocks in most every dredge haul after the first two, but not what we expected. One dredge haul was full of manganese nodules, some formed around a core of a single shark's tooth. We broke a few open. All of the ship's crew was out in the stern on their hands and knees sorting through the manganese nodules. The largest was about the size of an orange. Others were smaller, down to tiny sizes, about four centimeters in diameter. These hydrated manganese oxides were dirty little devils that left marks on our hands and clothes. The best-looking nodules or most exotic were packed in cotton batting. When they dry out, they tend to fall apart if not carefully packaged.

Our last dredge, as I recall, was on the Madagascar Ridge near the Mozambique Channel. When the chain bag came up on deck, lots of objects tinkled out on the deck—thousands of barnacle shells, all dead. I wondered how thick they were down there. There were certainly enough shells to suggest some sort of mass extinction. It is a shame that we couldn't get photographs at the dredge sites, but since there was only one cable, you couldn't have the large camera and the big dredge out at the same time. The camera was a large cone-shaped object with the top end cut off. It was meant to be poised a meter or two off the bottom. Sometimes there were good photos of rocks at the ocean bottom, including some sea creatures that wandered into the field of the photo, but at other times, just blank black film was developed. If the camera tipped over, the lens would stare into the dark water. We lost a camera on this expedition. Someone said, "There goes twelve thousand dollars."

We published several papers on these new rocks from the floor of the Indian Ocean in *Science* and the *Bulletin of the Geological Society of America*. Also, we sent a manuscript to *Geochemistry* in the Soviet Union. They published the paper in Russian and sent us a number of reprints. Soviet oceanographers were working all over the Indian Ocean, dredging, coring, and doing depth soundings. In fact, our first multicolored printed map of the underwater topography of the Indian Ocean was given to us by Soviet oceanographers. We could get along with them just fine, and we exchanged data with them constantly. We all became good friends. Why must our governments be such ardent enemies? I don't know.

Trawling

A big net was bundled up on the stern of *Argo,* between the cabins and the frame that lowered and raised the hoist at the end of the stern. Now and then a seaman or lab man would be mending on the net or dragging part of it around, but I didn't ask about it. I assumed it was for fishing.

The crew said that we were going to have to work for the biologists today even though they weren't on board. Were there biologists on board? No. However, when they plan these expeditions at Scripps, anyone with a good project can ask for and usually get ship time. And it turned out that this was the day when the people on board would do the biology experiment.

The weather had a lot to do with the project, because they were going to drag this big net behind the ship and catch creatures from one to three thousand meters down. They call this sort of marine prospecting a midwater trawl. It was a relatively calm day with a bit of sunlight. It was a good day for trawling.

Then the men started to struggle with that net. The thing was enormous, a great cone that started out with a fairly large opening with coarse netting. Farther along, the netting was finer and when two-thirds of the net was out and dragging behind, they screwed a four-liter jar on the end. It looked very much like a mason jar for preserving fruit. We were moving very slowly, and the men wanted the net to sink to about two thousand meters and gather whatever marine creatures were down there. It took well over an hour to get the net and cable into the ocean. They planned to drag it for at least an hour or more. I didn't pay enough attention to the technique until I could see what they were trying to do. And the most aggravating thing was, they don't announce what they are going to do next. A lot of the scientists assumed that I had been to sea before. No, I had not been to sea. I wanted to learn about everything. Even with the hoist doing most of the work, it required a lot of men to feed the net into the water.

Now that the net was out and sinking, we picked up just a little speed, but not more than three knots and perhaps less than that.

Were most of the deep sea creatures small enough that they would fit into the glass jar at the end of the net? Somehow, I visualized those ugly fish that I had seen in books as being big or at least medium-size, so what would come up? Several of the men said that they had trawled like this before and that interesting creatures came up in the jar.

Everyone was in the stern waiting. People always like to see creatures from the deep sea. We had a lot of flying fish, which were always active near the bow end of the ship when it was moving, but they were near-surface fish. These thin silvery fish leaped along beside the ship. Some fell onto the bow and died. They have a thin body and large filamentous fins. These fins make the flying fish far more exotic than a trout or bass. With their thin body and large, delicate fins, these fish were able to "fly" about fifty to two hundred feet or more. It was amazing how long they could stay out of the water on each leap. Now we were hunting for fish from several thousand meters down.

One man had a book of what looked like white blotting paper. This was thick absorbent paper that they put the specimens on, first to photograph them and then to put them into a jar of alcohol to preserve them and get them back to San Diego.

"Are you going to reel the net in soon?"

"Yes, soon."

Waiting. Everyone was acting like a child. Children get into the car and then ask immediately, "When are we going to get there?"

Bringing the net in did not seem quite as difficult as putting it into the water. The hoist man reeled in very slowly. The ship was stopped. And they reeled and reeled and dragged the net by hand into the huge pile from which it had come.

Finally, the end of the net, the closely woven part,

and the jar came into view. Careful—they don't want to break the bottle. It must be a tough glass considering the beating it takes. The bottle was full. Then the excitment started, with everyone crowding around.

Most of the specimens were fish—ugly little creatures. The largest was perhaps five centimeters long, and then there were all sizes down to ugly little babies. Most looked like closely related species. The adults had a bony head, too large for the body, which was slim and silvery. Many animals have cute babies, but not these fish. The infants had even larger heads relative to the body than the adults. The very small fish that were intact were about two centimeters long.

Most of the creatures were dead, but a few were still alive. It was a bad ride from hundreds of meters down to up here on the deck in the pale sunlight.

They laid the fish on the white paper and took the photos. They were hurrying so the creatures wouldn't dry out and blow away.

Someone said, "Celeste, hold this."

"What?" I really didn't want to hold any of these things.

"Take this little jellyfish." It was orange-red, about the size of a U.S. half-dollar, so it fit neatly into the palm of my hand. It was ALIVE. The little heart or whatever pulsed a few times and then went limp. It went into a jar of alcohol, too.

Other creatures were strange-looking shrimp, some worms with fins, and odds and ends, very different from anything I had ever seen. The only handsome creature was the little jellyfish.

Donovan

Argo came into Port Louis, Mauritius, two times during Expedition Circe. On the second trip into port, some of us were asked to join a geologic trip to Round Island. Jean Baissac was our host and guide. We were going to make the trip in his boat.

We left the yacht basin at Grand Baie on Mauritius at about 1000 hours and headed north to Round Island. The yacht basin had seen much better days. There was a bandstand, some run-down buildings, and rotting boats that could not be called yachts. Small sailboats were anchored about, one- or two-man sailboats. The Mauritians of English and French descent said they had sailboat races occasionally.

Baissac was an eighth-generation French Mauritian. He was a sugar planter, politician, and scientist, interested in all things geologic, oceanographic, biologic—everything. Baissac took us out in an old inboard motorboat. It had a small depth recorder in the bow that could be used as a fish-finder if there were schools of fish. Four of us came from *Argo*, and Baissac's nephew was along.

We were going to Round Island to see fossiliferous limestone beds that were interlayered with volcanic conglomerates. The limestone was deposited flat, or nearly flat, on the ocean floor and then tipped and raised above the water to form an island. Baissac's nephew had a rifle along. He wanted to shoot rabbits, which they had transplanted to the island. I made up my mind not to watch while the nephew went hunting for rabbits.

Then we were headed north-northeast under cloudy skies with quite a bit of wind. We passed small volcanoes that were about one to two thousand meters in diameter, and some were almost leveled by the pounding surf. Other volcanoes had split apart, and there we saw steep sea-cliffs. One side had fallen into the sea, and we could see into the throats of the volcanoes. All of the rocks were reddish oxidized alkali-rich basalts.

The ocean floor swells during volcano building, and after the eruptions cease, some of the volcanic cones sink and fall over at dizzy angles. It would be quite a sight watching the volcano on fast-forward here. Lava would bubble up, boil and steam, shoot chunks (volcanic bombs), lava, and ash into the air, then break open, spill out molten rock on the sea floor, and go dormant.

Baissac had an old canvas bag beneath his feet. He said he had our lunch in there. He was always thoughtful and gracious.

His little boat, about twenty-five feet long, rolled, pitched, and yawed. No one could get used to the motion, and we were wet most of the time. I moved closer to Baissac. It was drier on his bench, and I felt sick. If I kept busy talking to him, I might be okay.

A huge whale came alongside and rolled over near the little boat. What if the whale decided to roll under the boat? We would be scattered in the water, clutching a few sticks of wood of the boat. The whale disappeared, but it did serve to show us what puny creatures we were.

All the men from *Argo* were pale gray and quiet. One lay down on the other bench.

Baissac said "Celeste, we feed them now." Oh, boy, but yes, it is true, if you can eat and keep the stomach happy, you won't get sick. He had hard rolls, a chunk of butter, ham, and cheese. I cut and buttered the rolls, but I was too slow. He grabbed some rolls and helped me. Then we sliced the cheese and slapped the ham on the sandwich. When I passed the sandwiches around, some of the guys just shook their heads.

I said, "Yes, dammit, nibble on the food." They all tried and some tried harder than others. I grabbed a sandwich for myself. If you give up, you will be a mess.

As we munched away, Baissac told us an amazing story. During World War II, the sister ship to this one, filled with volunteers from Mauritius, sailed north to Egypt. They were going to join British forces in the North African campaigns, because Mauritius was under the British flag then. These men wanted to help. They sailed north along the East African coast for two thousand miles. The trip took them six or seven weeks, and they were short of food and water most of the time. They arrived safely, but they were too late and were not needed in the fighting. Some of the men stayed in Egypt, but most sailed back to Mauritius. They did have to stop a lot for fuel for the boat, and they had to evade the Germans who might be cruising along the coast. I assume this tale is true. But Baissac liked to tell me stories, because I believed everything. I didn't ask our men if they believed it. Surely they would not volunteer for such a trip considering how seasick they were after just one hour.

We arrived at Round Island, and there was no easy place to go ashore. One man stayed on board, and the others jumped ashore in the raging surf. I was last and I knew that I would fall in between the boat and the rocks on the island. There were thousands of little fish, what we called gobis at home. They were perched on their pectoral fins on the flatter rocks. For seconds they were out of the water, and then the next swell covered them. My guess is that they were feeding on tiny organisms in the water.

I said, "I will stay here in the boat. Don't feel you have to hurry back." I did want to stay in the boat. I did not want to go onto the island.

"No," Donovan said. "You jump when I tell you to do so, even if it looks wrong to you. You jump when I say, 'Jump'."

Oh, hell, I guess I had to try.

Donovan was part of the scientific crew, and he could do anything on board that had to be done. He didn't have to be brave in this situation.

Okay, I stood on the edge, and finally he shouted, "Jump!" He yelled when the boat was way below the landing place. It didn't look right, and I hesitated for several seconds. When I finally jumped, the boat was going up fast, and when I hit the rocks, I fell all over Donovan. Of course he collapsed, but I hung onto him and crawled over his body to the shore. I was weak from laughing, and we were both soaked in the waves. Donovan was not laughing.

"See, you should have left me in the boat." He didn't answer, but the weather was warm and we both dried out. I hope he wasn't hurt.

And after all of that and knowing that I am a clumsy clod, Donovan offered to get me ashore in Mozambique. This time we were coming off *Argo* onto a shore boat. The shore boat was going up and down next to *Argo*—the same situation, except that this time the waves were not as strong, but if I fell in that dirty-looking water in between the vessels, I might get mashed. Besides, I had to get off *Argo*, because this was the end of the journey at sea for me.

Donovan called, "Jump!" again. This time I was just a little bit better. I fell on him again, but we were both dry because we fell in a heap on the bottom of the shore boat.

When we got home to San Diego, I asked about Donovan. Was he okay? Yes, but a little while later, he gave up his job and went elsewhere.

Pilots

It was early morning and the ship was quiet. Yesterday, at sea, we could smell firewood burning, so we knew that we were close to the East African coast. Of course, we also knew that from the maps our scientists had. They were able to get better positions on latitude as we approached the coast.

Ships were all over, big ships, little ships, and sizes in between, but nothing as big as an oil tanker. All were anchored and the water was calm. In the midst of all the ships was a little shore boat labelled Pilotos. The pilot boat was anchored and rocking gently in the water. They appeared to be sleeping. Every ship was quiet. You don't want to rankle the pilots in the their boat. We waited. There was no way to get into Mozambique except with a pilot boat to lead us.

This part of the East African coast is what geologists call a drowned coast. It contained shifting sandbars, some with plants that looked like willows, and broad rivers with wide estuaries that flowed sluggishly into the ocean.

Then we were lucky. The Mozambique pilot radioed to *Argo* that we should follow the U.S. ship named *Christiana,* which would follow the pilot boat. Happily, we were second in line and in the first group of ships to go into port. The port was then called Lorenço Marques. Our captain asked me if I would like to watch us follow from the wheelhouse. "Oh, yes."

Our captain was seated in the chair on the starboard side, and I sat in the twin chair on the port side. Now we were moving and ahead was *Christiana,* with Corpus Christi, Texas printed on the stern—just like being at home. *Christiana* looked old and rusty, and it rode high in the water, as if it was empty.

It seemed to me that we were too close to the ship ahead. Several times, the crewman at the wheel looked at our captain as if he needed new instructions or wanted to reduce speed. I was horrified. I don't know how to run a ship, but I can feel when we are too close to something. I knew that we had to stay close to avoid sandbars, but there was one man watching from the stern of *Christiana* and he looked scared. We were so close that I could see his face clearly. Finally, our captain said "Reverse engines, ten degrees starboard," and we slowed and glided slightly past *Christiana.*

After that, we followed closely but at a much reduced speed. I had the feeling that our captain wanted to show us all that this old tub could go—if necessary, to the bottom.

Exit (Mozambique)

When we departed from *Argo,* I do remember that a young man in a white uniform came on board. He was sitting in the lounge, and now I know what he was doing. He was checking every passport for a valid visa for Mozambique. I didn't have a visa. I had planned to depart at Mauritius, where I did have a visa.

Somehow, I was hurried off the ship and didn't speak to the young official. Someone said, "Cook and Company will take care of you onshore."

Oceanographic vessels have agents in every port who supply food, fuel, water, towels, sheets, et cetera—everything you need to go on. The agents know the vessel is coming months, years, in advance.

Everyone who was getting off here went to a hotel to wait for a flight to South Africa to start home to San Diego. I asked, "Where is this place that I should go for a visa or whatever?" The chief scientist took me to the office, and it was lunchtime. The Cook and Company office here was run by Frenchmen, not by Portuguese. They asked us if we would like to join them for lunch.

"Yes, delighted, but what should I do . . . ?" Someone shushed me and we went upstairs to the private dining room. From the second floor we could see all over the city. It was large and built on flat land with just one small ridge with expensive homes. This soggy, sodden estuary must have been the perfect breeding ground for malaria, yellow fever, and other tropical diseases.

The dining room was an elegant room with a table set with fine linen and silver. They had a wine rack larger than any I had ever seen before. When we sat down, every chair or diner had his or her own servant standing behind the chair. I was mesmerized.

Each course required a clean plate and another glass for the next wine, but I didn't know if the first course was the only one. It was cauliflower with a cheese sauce, topped with large shrimp. I took too much and had to eat all of it, then the plate was whisked away and there followed at least six courses plus dessert—every course with the proper wine. I can't drink much. One glass is my limit. I didn't try to keep up with the drinking, but I drank more than I should have. The servant behind me was always ready with the next glass. I put my hand over my glass, and the servant understood that. After this incredible meal, which lasted almost three hours, I decided to take a long walk. I had a headache from drinking, and my back was sore from sitting such a long time. How do those businessmen get anything done? However, they were probably thinking ahead to more business from U.S. research vessels.

At that time, Mozambique was held by the Portuguese. They were at the end of the line, but they were hanging on. The Portuguese flag, which we flew when we entered port, was the oldest flag in the world. We looked all through the books trying to find an older flag, but couldn't find one. The flag of Portugal is red and green with an elaborate crest.

I walked past a school, and the children were just getting out. They were very handsome children with olive-colored skin, and a lot of them had blue eyes, a lovely combination. The Portuguese were good at living with the natives wherever they had a colony.

But there were armed soldiers everywhere—at the cafés on the street, at the schools, at the hotels, on street corners, on the docks, everywhere.

Someone said, "Here, look at *Newsweek*." In the index was listed an article about Salazar, the Portuguese dictator. When we turned to the pages where the article should be, it was neatly shaved out with a razor. The news was so bad from back home in Portugal that they didn't want to spread it around here.

I bought a simple dress and some shoes that were clean. Everyone had to wait for another day, because few airlines have this place on their route. Cashew nuts were the main cash crop. The hotel had displays of one-kilo to twenty five-kilo cans. The creatures that I thought were ocean shrimp were actually fresh water crayfish, very good, but big plates of them were served at every meal—crayfish and a salad of turnips and carrots. I don't know where the men in the private dining room bought their food. The other big cash crop was weekend tourists from South Africa. These pale-skinned people came over to gamble and watch the nightclub shows in which black people starred.

The next day, we went to the airport. I remember this airport for a lot of reasons. The toilets in the ladies' room were not bolted to the floor, and when I sat down, the toilet started to fall over. Sit down very carefully! I bought a ticket to Johannesburg. We got in line to get on the plane, which had propellers, no jets. Okay, I was sick of this place. Then a man from the hotel came hurrying up to the passenger desk. I had given my boater shoes to the maid in my room, and they wanted to know if she had stolen my shoes.

"No, of course not. I gave her the shoes." The whole colony was a pile of corruption, and they were concerned over a pair of shoes.

Then the immigration official looked at my passport. He said, "You have no entry mark. If you did not enter, how can you exit?" He was a short man, and as he scanned my passport he stroked his mustache and murmured, "Um," going from page to page.

I explained as best I could, and everyone tried to help me explain that I did not have a visa and had no entry stamp because I had missed the official on *Argo* and then forgot to ask at Cook and Company, and on and on. I admit the explanations sounded feeble. But I was forty eight-years old, a female scientist, and certainly not a terrorist.

The official said, "Go sit down over there. You can't leave."

I sat down and felt numb. My mind drifted back to that damn hotel. They were building an office building next door and there was never a quiet moment, but if I had to sit in it until someone got me out of Mozambique, okay. The engines started and everyone waved out the windows . . . good-bye.

At what must have been the very last moment, the official said "Get on the plane." He ordered the plane door opened, and I ran for it.

I don't have an entry or an exit stamp from Mozambique. I was never there!

The Moon

Jim Arnold of the chemistry faculty phoned our laboratory one day in 1965 and asked if we would like to work on moon samples. He elaborated—we would have to write a proposal and submit it to NASA.

Al usually wrote the proposals and I typed the first draft, but he was out of the country. I was trying to think very fast and I was silent too long, because Arnold said, "Are you there?"

"Yes. . . . I am thinking."

I was thinking rapidly. What if the moon was covered with meteorites, both nickel-iron and stony meteorites or perhaps a mixture of the two? There are many types of meteorites, and all are very difficult to analyze for major elements and some minor elements, which is what we would propose to do. Many scientists thought the surface of the moon was plastered with meteorites.

For example, if any rock or meteorite contains a lot of iron and I made a conventional fusion in a platinum crucible, the iron would combine with the platinum. I would ruin the moon rock and the crucible. We could not use our conventional methods to analyze moon samples. We would have to modify our analytical procedures.

This was 1965, or perhaps 1966, and no samples from the moon were expected at all until 1969. The U.S. finally landed on the moon on July 20, 1969. We usually don't plan that far ahead.

Still, I said, "Yes."

"Fine," Arnold said. "Your proposal must be ready in ten days and will be attached to ours. There will be five proposals from this university, and we are ready with ours."

One of the proposals was to look for organic material (life?). Others would do isotopic analyses to date the moon materials. Was the moon formed as a sister planet to Earth, or did the Earth capture the moon? Lots of questions were up in the air. We would do quantitative chemical analyses of most major elements (Si, Al, Fe, Ca, and Mg) and some of the more useful minor elements (Ti, Mn, Na, K, and so on).

Arnold was most interested in Na (sodium) and K (potassium). The assumption was that many of these lighter elements would be lost on a body as small as the moon. Solar winds might lash the moon and sweep these lighter elements off the surface.

Two happy occurrences came together for us. We had worked a lot on basalts, in lava flows, of the oceans. These oceanic rocks had a very unique composition, not unlike that of certain basaltic achondrites (meteorites). And the other bit of luck, and the most important, was that the United States sent an unmanned spacecraft to circle the moon. One instrument was going to give the rough composition of the dark, flat areas of the moon. These dark areas are the maria, the seas, of the early astronomers.

From the X-ray fluorescence device that measured some areas of the moon, the predominant rock was another unique basalt, a titanium-rich basalt. I wrote the proposal as if I knew what we were doing. But the skewed composition, with so much titanium, would be a big problem in gravimetric chemical analyses.

A reporter from the *San Diego Union* called and asked for interviews with people who planned to analyze moon rocks. I told him that I was ready for anything. I was joking, of course, but the article was printed on the front page of the *Union* and the last line read: "Mrs. Engel is ready for anything." I had to go all over explaining my way out of that statement. If I could have done so, I would have purchased all copies of the *Union* and destroyed them.

Then I forgot about the moon and went back to work on rocks of the oceanic crust.

We can see basaltic rocks everywhere. There are many different varieties—the Hawaiian Islands, Iceland, and the Columbia River basalts of the northwestern United States, to point out a few.

In the Hawaiian Islands, basalts erupt from fissures or cracks along the flanks of the huge volcanoes. We have all seen the yellow-red fire fountains on the TV set at home. The melted rock flows down mountain sides, engulfing trees, farms, highways and now and then a house or two. That is how the oceanic basalts form, as melted magma from far beneath the surface erupted into valleys or in rifts in the bottom of the ocean. At ocean-spreading centers (rifts) basalt erupts into the cold water and the surface of the rock cools instantly to a smooth black glass containing crystals of white feldspar.

I brought some samples of basaltic glass dredged from the western Indian Ocean back home in my suitcase. They were small globs, like black pearls. When I reached customs in the United States in Los Angeles, the agent in charge argued with me that they were "jewels." Well, of course, they were jewels to me, expensive jewels, but not like rubies and diamonds. We weren't going to sell them. I finally did get these basaltic gems through customs—free, but not without a big squabble.

Several years passed and finally the astronaut Armstrong stepped onto the moon and said, "One small step for man . . . "and we could see his footprints in the moon dust, which looked like the dust in a coal mine.

First, Armstrong and his colleague had to put up the flag of the United States. It was a solid aluminum flag made so it would appear to fly in the wind. No wind there. Back on earth, the scientist were yelling to themselves and to others, "Pick up samples! . . . Pick up rocks! . . . Grab a bagful of the black dust!"

All of us were afraid that they might have to leave in a hurry, possibly immediately, so they should collect as many samples as possible at the landing site and then put up the flag. Armstrong had orders, of course, so he stuck the flag in the surface. Okay. Then they started to collect rock samples and the two astronauts put out an array of instruments to measure moonquakes and so on.

I think that Armstrong had pockets for samples in the knees of his spacesuit. I heard that and it may be garbage, but the mission was very successful. The men returned to earth with a lot of rock samples, and they and the samples were put into isolation rooms. Perhaps the moon had strange bacteria that would finish man off.

We had to be very careful. Strange—that did not worry me at all. I could not believe anything could survive in the intense heat and cold of the moon. Man has never been to a more sterile place.

Now special security started in our laboratory at Scripps. We had to have a large file cabinet of heavy metal, locked with a four-digit number sequence. The cabinet had to be locked whenever I left the laboratory. Everyone wanted a piece of the moon.

The four-digit number was so complicated—four turns left past zero to 33, and on and on. I had to write the combination of numbers everywhere. I put it on sticky paper and stuck it under my desk. I wrote it on a tiny piece of paper and folded it and put it into a beaker on the top shelf out of sight. I wrote it backwards and kept it in my driver's license and in several other places that I can't remember now.

Now we were ready.

Then, NASA would not mail the samples. Someone had to go to Houston to pick up the samples. They didn't send me because I couldn't remember the numbers on my lock.

From this first moon landing, *Apollo 11*, we had five samples. Two looked alike through the milky plastic containers. They were the black dust. Then there were three small fragments of rock. Each sample weighed about five grams. I usually didn't have to work on samples this small. One mistake, and the samples would be gone forever. We had to dissolve or fuse the moon rocks in order to determine the amounts of various elements. Our samples would be destroyed.

On this first group of samples, NASA did not provide thin sections. We always want to look through the rock in thin section. In a thin section, we could identify the translucent minerals and also see how much of the rock was composed of opaque oxides and sulfides of metals. A lot of opaque minerals would mean a lot of trouble for us.

The black dust was so fine that particles would creep along paper, glass, and anything else we touched to it. But we did make our own thin section with a little of the dust smeared on a glass slide in immersion oil. Then we covered the dust with a round cover glass. So we wasted a few milligrams, but there it was, dust from the moon, winking back at us under the microscope.

All of the minerals and fragments were gorgeous, pristine, fresh minerals. They sparkled like tiny jewels.

On the Earth we have water and gases that attack all rocks. I have never seen a truly fresh rock except from the moon. It spoils work on the altered, oxidized, and hydrated minerals in even the best preserved rocks on Earth.

We were very careful with such precious and expensive samples. If one gets too nervous, one could spill or goof up for sure. I decided to use only half the sample needed for various chemical determinations. That worked fairly well. I wanted to determine titanium with one-half an aliquot, because it was so abundant, and sodium and potassium, which were low, with a full portion. I saved enough sample to do everything two times. We used all of the samples. And, most important, we didn't spill anything.

Sample 10084, the fine black dust, was distributed to five different chemical groups. Na (sodium) was: 0.33 (us), 0.33 (Denver), 0.29 (Canada), 0.33 (Finland), and 0.32 (England) in weight percent, so the spread was 0.33

to 0.29 for chemists in four different countries, all using different methods on five splits of the same sample. Arnold was pleased. We were, too.

Actually, the splits could not be identical, although I am certain that NASA took special care to take the splits from a well-mixed larger sample. Potassium (K) was very low in 10084; the values for K, in weight percent, were very close: 0.08 to 0.11. Titanium (Ti) was so high, 6 to 7 weight percent, that it precipitated everywhere, in every solution. Titanium was a big headache for me.

I was probably the least experienced of all the chemists, but I didn't know who else had samples. Yes, I knew that Denver would have samples because they were very good, Vicki Smith and Lee C. Peck. Their work was always better than mine. But we all came out with very similar values, which meant that the NASA teams in Texas would have good "standards" to calibrate their costly analytical X-ray rigs, which were just coming into use for the analysis of rocks and minerals.

We had moon samples from *Apollo 12, 14, 15,* and *16*. *Apollo 13* did not get to the moon. I believe their oxygen tanks exploded and the men barely returned alive. Al didn't care for the project at all, because he always wants to collect his own rocks. It is more fun if the samples are your own. I did enjoy *Apollo 16* because one of Al's ex-students was the geologist on that expedition. I always wondered, as I viewed each sample, if Harrison Schmitt picked up that particular rock on the moon. At least, that way we were attached to the project—through a student.

After the NASA teams had good standard analyses of moon rocks, they cut us out of the programs. All the chemists who needed to dissolve samples were out of business. I was glad to get out of it anyway. The only huge thrill was seeing the moon fragments under the microscope for the first time. Otherwise, in a jar or a vial, the rocks looked just like rocks I had seen before. Most important, I could throw out that difficult lock with the crazy combination. But if you turn up a chair at Scripps, you might see my tiny numbers for the combination lock written under the seat.

Helen

Helen Raitt and I were going to New Caledonia. Her husband was a guest geophysicist on a Russian research vessel that was coming into Noumea. We knew some of the Russians on board, and Helen loved to travel in the South Pacific.

For years I had been reading everything I could find on the geology of the circum-Pacific. It is an enormous area, and of course I missed a lot of papers.

New Caledonia had deposits of iron, nickel, cobalt, gold, and silver. The islands were annexed by France in 1853. The French Colonial Geological Survey completed most of the early mapping of the islands, and their work was good. Much later, when plate tectonics became the rage, everyone hypothesized that the deposits were part of the ocean crust that had been thrust up over an old island arc that is now New Caledonia.

Helen and I left early during the Christmas recess at school so that we didn't have to hurry to Noumea but would have more time to see Hawaii and Fiji. Helen had a friend in Honolulu who was a sculptor and taught at the University of Hawaii. The flight from San Diego to Honolulu was five hours long instead of the usual four hours. The pilot said that we had an unusually strong headwind. Before jet airplanes were developed, the air trip to Hawaii had what was called a point of no return. If the plane was running out of fuel early in the flight, then the pilot should turn around and ride a tailwind to the U.S. mainland. If he didn't return, then I guess he had to hope he could make it to Hawaii. Of course, that was only going west. This point of no return fascinated me for years. When I was young, I thought there was a sign hanging out there somewhere in the Pacific sky that warned pilots.

We stayed in a hotel near the beach, and we went to the shopping areas looking for colorful muumuus to wear for New Year's Eve.

Helen's friend, a woman sculptor, had a small house on a hill overlooking the lights of Honolulu, and the house was filled with her work. She had a delightful Italian or French accent, but I can't remember her name. It seemed cool to cold in Hawaii. Both Helen and I were freezing in the dampness.

In 1970, American Airlines was initiating new flights to Fiji. We always tried to use U.S. carriers, if we could. This flight was on a new Boeing 707, and there were only seven passengers on board. After we were in the air, we could move about into any group of seats we wished. Helen had a weak heart, so she tried to sleep a lot. I am certain that she was afraid to go anywhere alone. Tonight would be New Year's Eve in the Fiji Islands.

When Helen and I landed at Nadi, we were met at the plane by black women, American Airline employees, who were holding umbrellas for us. It was cloudy and a light rain was falling. I noticed here that the black women spoke the King's English. There wasn't a trace of what people call a black accent, as we have in our southern United States. Now, I assume that our blacks learned their accent from the southern whites and not vice versa.

Fiji was in the midst of a building boom of luxury hotels. Most were built by various airlines. A giant was rising next to our hotel. It was owned by Quantas. The air terminal was new and decorated with Fijian weapons—hatchets, axes, nooses, clubs, bows, lances, and arrows—but there were also a few specimens of celebration bowls and marriage adornments and the like. No shrunken heads or scalp locks. I always wonder why men have to make tools to kill each other.

Helen and I each had our own room at the hotel. The place was relatively new and air-conditioned, but they couldn't keep the place dried out. There was a huge swimming pool and no one was swimming, so I took a chance. I remember floating on my back and looking at the sky, which was cloudy and angry-looking. After I looked up close at the color of the water in the pool, green, I got out, too. Who knows what creatures were living in that water, which was a perfect culture for any kind of bacteria—virus, worm, or whatever?

At 2200 hours on New Year's Eve, Helen and I dressed in our new clothes and went to the dining room–lounge affair. No one was there except a few members of the crew from the airline. We sat around for some time, and then Helen became tired and we went to bed. It was not until years later, when I was looking at a map of the eastern Pacific, that I realized that Fiji was on the other side of the International Date Line. We lost New Year's Eve in a wink when we crossed the date line.

The next morning at breakfast, someone put a newspaper on our table and Helen and I read that the weather in the area was dominated by a strong hurricane. The map on the front page looked as if we were in the hurricane or would be soon. That's why the weather was cloudy, but we had no wind, just a lot of rain. While Helen wrote letters and postcards, I took a long walk along narrow tarvia roads. Most of the people in Nadi were dark-complexioned and friendly. The town was full of flowers, everything was blooming, including one vine I knew from California—the Copa de Oro. Here the blossoms were huge, yellow and about the size and shape of a small trumpet.

From Fiji to New Caledonia, Helen and I were on a French airline, the southern arm of Air France, UTA, or some such. While we were sitting in the plane waiting to take off, a Quantas airliner was boarding next to us. Every Australian who could walk and carry a bag had four bottles of liquor. The heavy paper bags were made for this stop. Some of the Quantas passengers ran in and out of the terminal at least twice. I guess the infants were allowed a bag of alcohol also.

When we first saw New Calendonia, Helen said, "Look, the ocean is red." I knew then that the hurricane had passed by here and not long ago. The red color was due to the lateritic soils that were carried by the flooding rivers into the ocean. The airport was a long way from Noumea—at least, it seemed long to me. Instead of just dumping us at the airport, the airline had arranged to take us into Noumea in cars and trucks. When we came to large flooding streams, we were herded onto a World War II amphibious landing craft. Those French stewardesses in their white uniforms were all splashed with muddy red water. Some passengers said they wouldn't get onto that thing, but they finally did. We crossed about a quarter-mile of rushing red water, and I am not certain if we were floating or riding on the bottom.

At the junction of two red streams was a statue of Christ facing us, with arms outstretched. It was eerie. The statue appeared to be standing on the water. Some passengers became very excited and wanted to stop there for photos. But we didn't, we kept crawling along.

The airline crew was heroic. A lot of the passengers were old and afraid of this amphibious craft. It was a U.S. World War II machine. The United States left millions of tons of war material, great piles of metal, on the islands or rusting in lagoons. Everything was rotting, except this thing, which managed to rumble along.

Finally we arrived at Noumea and made it to the hotel. The grounds around the hotel were roped off because coconuts were falling out of trees. The gardens were all ripped up. Plants were stripped of leaves, and everything was soaked.

Helen and I were put into rooms in the hotel annex. They said there would be breakfast on the lawn at the edge of the ocean the next morning.

I turned off the lights and lay down to go to sleep. It was such a busy, exciting day that we were exhausted. When the lights went out, giant cockroaches rushed around in the dark and many crawled all over the bed. I bashed some of them with my shoe, but they were very fast.

Helen and I did eat breakfast at the hotel near the ocean. They gave us fruit juice with rolls and coffee. Helen asked about for a place to dine that night. She loved to hunt for French cooking. We dined at a small place where the door and windows were open. Vines grew from outside, through the windows, and hung from the ceiling. The diners at the table next to us were all excited because a large fruit bat about ten inches long was hanging by its feet and making its way slowly along the vines. It was begging for food.

Helen said, "Oh, it is coming to us."

"Helen, don't you talk to that thing."

The next day, Helen and I went to rent a car at Hertz. When we gave the address as University of California, the owner went into a tirade about the deadbeats from the university. He claimed he had to fly to Berkeley to get his money back from one rental agreement. We were not from the Berkeley campus, so finally he rented us an old VW Bug.

Now we were ready to see the country. I hoped to see outcrops of rocks along the roads. Instead we saw roadcuts of lateritic soil and millions of Norfolk Island pines, the lacy trees that people and banks have for indoor plants back in the States. These pines were the weed of New Caledonia.

The houses in New Caledonia were built on pillars of concrete block for ventilation from below, and the first floor was an open garage, almost always with the wash hanging out on lines. Did it ever stop raining there?

The roads were narrow and winding, and at every curve in the road, there was a car, wrecked. Some were leaning up against trees. Others were out in the weeds. When we finally got up to thirty-five miles per hour, the back end of our VW started to shake and shiver. It was very scary. We took it back to Hertz, and he gave us something else that was almost as bad. I could see why the Berkeley crowd had not paid him.

At Noumea, the government funded an oceanographic institute of sorts. It was a beginning, and the main thrust was to study sea life. The man in charge was a big surprise. He had come from studying snow and ice (glaciers) in Switzerland and settled down here with a young Polynesian wife in a beautiful house. They had two handsome children. He also had a wife and two children back in Switzerland.

Helen and I were asked to have lunch with them, and we dressed up, in dresses, stockings, and shoes. The hostess wore about three meters of colorful fabric wrapped about her body sort of in the style of a diaper below the waist and an off-the-shoulder drape above the waist. She was slim and exotic, and she could curl her legs under her body when she sat down on a chair. I was not moving at all, just sitting, and perspiration poured off me. What a dreadful climate—very hot and humid. You would have to run around naked to survive here.

Their home had no glass in the windows. Vines grew into the open spaces, climbed about the ceilings, and grew out again. Everything was blooming. I was so curious that I finally asked, "How do you put that dress, uh, that thing, on?" She demonstrated by whipping off the outfit. She wore no bra, just panties under it. Then she went for a stack of fabric—hand-painted prints, pinks, purples, yellow, orange, every tropical color one can imagine. Her wardrobe was stacked up on shelves like bath towels, and she could get dressed and select earrings in about four minutes flat. She didn't wear shoes, at least not at home.

Well, we did see a lot of New Caledonia, but the Russian vessel radioed from Norfolk Island that it would not come into Noumea. They had a change of plans. Helen's husband was trying to arrange transportation from Norfolk Island to New Caledonia. Helen would have to wait one extra day.

I went home and as fast as possible. I guess I am the only person alive who has little love for the South Pacific.

Bill Otto

When Al and I first met Bill Otto, he was working with Prof. Chester Stock at the California Institute of Technology in Pasadena. Stock was a vertebrate paleontologist, one who studies fossil animals that have backbones. I can't recall which fossil vertebrates they were working on when we first met, but I think they were the animals from the La Brea Tar Pits in Los Angeles. Bill's job was to extract from the rock, clay, and tar and to reconstruct the skeletons of fossil vertebrates from mouse-size to elephant-size. After cleaning and rebuilding each bone, he joined them together to complete an entire skeleton of the creature in a lifelike pose. It was an art, demanding and tedious.

Oil seeps like La Brea are natural animal traps. Where oil is near the surface, it commonly oozes out, loses some of its moisture, and becomes a gummy black mass of tar. When a bit of rainwater covers this tar-rich surface, animals step in to drink and get stuck and usually die of exhaustion from floundering about trying to get free. Predators come to feed on the trapped animals, and they also get stuck. Eventually the tar deposits were filled with the bones of all the animals that lived and flourished in the area. Tar is a good preservative for skeletons. The La Brea tar pits were nature's storehouse for an incredible variety of prehistoric creatures. All this occurred about twenty thousand years ago. At that time, the area near Wilshire Boulevard in Los Angeles was a rich savanna grassland where thousands of animals and birds lived on what is now a teeming, bustling city of people, streets, houses, and giant office buildings. There are other tar pits, but the La Brea site is one of the best and now it is covered, protected from damage, and has a museum with models of animals and paintings to show visitors what went on there not so many years ago. The tar pits left a rich history for us to study. Bill Otto did a lion's share of the fossil reconstructions.

Otto also did some work in conjunction with the Los Angeles County Museum. That museum now has most of the animals from the tar pits on display—that is, the reconstructed animals. They also have thousands of extra parts of the La Brea animals—odd ribs, skulls, teeth, leg bones, and vertebrae.

At Caltech Otto worked in a huge room with big tables. Whole animal skeletons or parts of them were stretched out in trays and racks. Partial to complete reconstructions were on some of the tables. The first thing that struck me about Otto was how neat he was. Every tool and substance had a place and was in its place. And every job he tackled was done with precision and care.

One day I went into Otto's lab and asked, "What's this?" He had a large, flat piece of sedimentary rock with the fossilized bones of an animal in it. I think it was some sort of cat, not a saber tooth cat, but a cat a bit smaller. Or it may have been a small horse, I can't remember. That was many years ago. The rock was only about 8 inches thick. The animal died and then was covered with mud which hardened into rock. In the process, it was compressed to almost flat.

"How are you going to get it out of there and reconstruct a skeleton from a flat animal?" I asked.

Otto said, "It will take time, but I will do it."

Months later, when I looked in again, there it was, standing upright and filled out. All the bones were in place. Where bones were missing, as in the vertebrae,

Otto had fashioned new bones and painted or stained them so the whole thing looked "real," as if he had every bone in the first place. They had to move some of the big creatures around with a crane hung from the ceiling.

Naturally, Otto had a great stream of visitors, because everyone is interested in animals from the past, especially the exotic menagerie that Stock and Otto had.

Otto and a man named Ted at the LA County Museum reconstructed all of the animals from the tar pits—camels, saber-toothed cats, bears, vultures, wolves, antelope, sloths, and many more. I think they had a thousand extra fangs from saber-toothed carnivores. The tar pits contained a stunning array of animals and so many different kinds. I must go back there sometime and look again. The tar is still there, and gas bubbles rise to the surface and plop out into the air.

There was a reconstructed Devonian "fish;" a big ugly thing, with giant eye sockets. It was set into a matrix of plaster and hung on the wall of the geology building stairwell. The whole thing must have weighed half a ton.

Bill and I were walking down the stairs one day and I asked, "One of your pets?"

"Yes," he said.

He did all sorts of creatures. But I don't think he ever did a human. He liked animals much better. However, if we walked on the beach at lunch, he commented on all the human females in bikinis.

When Stock died, Bill wanted to work for someone else. He especially liked to work on meticulous jobs, but I am certain that he could have spent his life on fossil vertebrates. Bill was a sculptor, too, and his many beautiful works lay mostly hidden at his home. Just now and then he would show me something he had made, and I was enchanted with everything he created. One of the geologists at Caltech brought Bill a big chunk of lavender lepidolite-rich rock. He carved a sleeping Madonna head from that. He did a fighting bull of welded tuff, volcanic rock, and I wanted that, too. He did a pair of squirrels out of howlite, a white borate-rich rock with brown swirls in the white. The brown streaks ran up the tails of the squirrels. Bill was a genius in rock sculpture. He also made small-scale models and molds of prehistoric animals, which were then cast in bronze. I saw those animals for sale at most major natural history museums. But he didn't want to be a full-time sculptor.

Finally, we asked if Bill could work one week for us in our lab. His care and precision were the traits we wanted for analytical work. On alternate weeks, Bill would switch gears and work for the invertebrate paleontologist. Eventually, Bill became a lot more involved in my lab and worked with me full-time. He was the person who kept our analytical work alive. He prepared all the rocks and minerals for us. We could trust his work. He never messed up or mixed samples or stopped short of a thorough job.

At first Bill complained, "Your work is all destructive. You are crushing and grinding up the rocks, while I used to put everything together." I know he felt terrible about that, but we had to crush the rocks to separate each mineral. All of the geologists tried to bring him beautiful rocks, but rock is heavy. When we were working on the Leadville limestone in Colorado, we planned to bring him a chunk from the Yule quarry, where a part of the limestone was reconstituted (metamorphosed) to a white marble. We know how heavy rock is and we could never get a really huge hunk because we had to carry it for several miles. Bill carved a polar bear on an ice flow from that piece of marble. It was magnificent. I wanted to buy it, if he would sell, but we didn't have enough money at the time. However, we do have an owl he made of basalt. It is lovely.

Then we moved from Pasadena to La Jolla, California, and thank God Bill came with us. If he had not come with us, our laboratory would have collapsed long before it did. His help was everything to us.

Bill also did some extra jobs of all kinds. Every scientist at Scripps and UCSD had their eyes on him. One day I went into his lab where he prepared all our samples, and he had two rocks about the size of grapefruits.

"What are you doing?"

"Oh, this is a meteorite from Professor Arnold's group. Arnold borrowed the meteorite, and he wants a copy of it. I am making a copy."

It was a stony meteorite with a glassy exterior that was sort of a mottled shade of brown, but there were colors from raw sienna to deep brown on the surface. There Bill was with a perfect copy of the original meteorite and he was painting the exterior of the copy. I couldn't tell one from the other unless I picked them up. The plaster copy was lighter in weight than the real thing. Otherwise, if I had to choose by just looking, I could not have told the copy from the original. He did other things like that, but he didn't show me most of his artistic work. Bill had a terrible disposition on Mondays. I learned that very slowly, and usually he was angry with me on Monday. By Tuesday he was okay again. We couldn't tell if he hated to come back to work or if his weekend had been awful.

In the laboratory at La Jolla, Bill began to help me more and more, with complex jobs. When we were doing ferric iron on a rock, he boiled the sample in hydrofluoric and sulfuric acid in a platinum crucible while I raced around to make the titrating solution and grab the crucible with platinum tongs when he was ready. We had a lot of little accidents, but they were usually my fault. One day I spilled nitric acid on the concrete floor and I didn't think I had hit anything until I felt my legs start to burn.

"Close your eyes!" I shrieked. "I am going to have to rip off my stockings and underwear!"

Bill was very clean and tidy. I had to try to live up to his standards. It was common for us to hit our heads together both trying to grab a kimwipe or a piece of lint or a bit of glass off the floor. We almost knocked each other out—hitting heads like that. And I had to remember while weighing something or when pouring acids that he might, he just might, throw an empty container into our metal wastebaskets. Of course, he was ready for the big crash in a silent room, but I was not. I am certain that I scared him, too. He just didn't tell me about it. When he was sawing a rock with a diamond-edged saw, I did not come up behind him or touch him or speak to him. I tried to leave him alone or come in from the side so he could see me. He could have cut off his precious fingers if startled.

In our super-clean lab, we even washed our floors on hands and knees. The glassware was sparkling and the platinum vessels were glowing all the time.

When Bill retired, I tried to carry on alone for almost two years, but the laboratory and equipment started to fall apart. The salt of the sea air corroded everything. I retired, too.

Bill was reticent about his own life. I lost track of him—he stopped writing. Now I don't know where he is.

They Don't See the Rocks

We see what we look for. We are blind to important things we do not know about.

When I am traveling by automobile in the U.S., I look at the rocks in the road cuts and out on the horizon. Then when I stop along the side of the road to let my dog sniff in the weeds, I push around the pebbles along the side of the road with my foot. I try to identify all the pebbles. Then I will watch for a quarry or gravel pit that the road department used for the road materials. At first glance, I can tell if the crushed rocks or pebbles in the road matrix are sedimentary or igneous-metamorphic rocks. Most road departments look for a source of sedimentary rocks because they are softer and easier to crush. And since rock is heavy, road builders don't want to transport material from far away. They look for a local source.

I learn a lot about rocks by looking at them from a car or in a road cut. In a lot of places I can't get out of the car and look as we used to do. The roads are fenced, and on interstate highways you can't stop anyway or you will be arrested or killed.

Last year, I was driving with a female friend. We were driving two cars from San Diego to Montana. It is a dull drive for me because I've made it many times, but I thought I would try to make it interesting to Regina. She was behind me in a pickup.

When we came near an eroded spire of volcanic rock, I didn't stop, but I pointed with my whole arm out of the window so that Regina would look also. I wanted her to see that majestic column of rock. The volcanic rock had cooled into symmetrical columnar joints. It was every bit as handsome as the Devil's Post Pile or similar features in Yellowstone Park, but smaller. Next we came to a playa (dry lake) with a bit of water in it and a perfect mirage of the distant hills. I pointed to that, over the top of the car, to the right. I planned to explain these features to her when we stopped for gasoline.

Half an hour later when we stopped, Regina said, "I saw that old wrecked car. Why were you pointing at that?" and "Were you pointing to the road that went over the mountains to Searchlight?" She didn't see the rock types or geological formations that I hoped to explain to her. She didn't see the rocks at all. They were not a part of her world. Rocks are everywhere. We live on a great sphere of rock, the Earth. When we die, the living bury us in it. Yet we rarely look at our home or try to learn much about it. Rocks are the landscape clothed in places by plants or covered with concrete.

Why should Regina look at rocks? After all, when she gets home and works in her garden, she has to get rid of rocks because they are in the way. She carts them off in her wheelbarrow to a pile at the edge of the yard. Her yard is surrounded by piles of rocks, which are fragments of a once immense chain of mountains.

For years I drove past beds of white volcanic tuff in Nevada. I was going to stop one of these days and look at it, I thought. This same material is ground up to make scouring powder to clean sinks in kitchens and baths. Then one summer day, I did stop and collected a beautiful big piece of white layered tuff. It had been deposited in water, in a lake or a sea, when volcanoes were belching clouds of ash into the air. I placed this handsome specimen near the door of our house, and although this ash is snow white and very distinctive, no one ever asked, "What is that?" Many adults don't look at rocks, unless they are told to do so by signs. But children, who are curious about everything, love to collect rocks and minerals. I have many small friends who store their rocks and minerals in old coffee cans. Then they dump their treasures in the dust and ask me to identify them. Their parents have not learned enough to identify rocks or how they formed, even though they live on a big round rock complex.

Years ago we made a trip to the Black Hills to visit a geologist who was working on banded gneisses. He took us into quarries of the Black Hills pegmatites. I have never seen such huge crystals in my life. I tried to haul off a sheet of mica as large as the top of a coffee table, but I couldn't get it into the car. There were crystals of beryl (Be, Al silicate) as large as big pine tree trunks. Obviously, I couldn't get specimens of them. Finally, I decided to take a handful of the broken stuff at my feet. The pegmatite crystals in the Black Hills were so enormous and stunning that I yearned for a railroad flatcar to help me cart off a few twenty-foot crystals.

At Caltech, a gem collector named Svoboda, who traveled between Europe and South America, used to visit Dick Jahns, one of our colleagues. One day Svoboda laid out an array of cut gems on black velvet, all semiprecious, as I recall: tourmalines, zircons, garnets, various forms of silica—tigereye, amethyst, rose and smokey quartz—beryl, spodumene, and others. I was stunned and stupid. Why didn't I buy something?

All of Svoboda's gems were large and gorgeous, but we were not interested in gems as objects of research. Or rather, Al told me that we were not interested in gems because they formed less than one-thousandth of one percent of the Earth and the hell with them.

It is far more likely that I will want specimens of

rocks, even banded gneisses, than gems to hang around my neck. I took Al to his dentist in Montana, and the dentist had his place landscaped with evergreens and tumbled colored sandstones from the Belt Formation. I looked all around and then stole five pebbles in shades of green, red, gray, and white. Each showed in minute detail the thin layers of sand deposited after each season, or storm over 1,000 million years ago.

We now live for about seven months of the year on the edge of the Idaho Batholith in western Montana. All batholiths contain a lot of granitic rocks. When we dug out the basement, we had to move all those surplus cobbles and small boulders somewhere else. Each one that I picked up was identified by me—pegmatitic granite, gneissic granite, granodiorite, granitized metasediment. I didn't mean to identify the rock; it just happened. Sometimes I can produce an instant chemical analysis in my head. That is ridiculous. All of these granitic rocks were dirty pink or gray, but now and then I found a black amphibolite that contained wine-red garnet. I hauled the better specimens of amphibolite to the house for a future black rock garden. Does anyone want a garden of black rocks?

These dark metamorphic rocks, amphibolites, with amphibole crystals that sparkle in the sun and contain wine-red garnets, are still exciting to me. We worked on amphibolite rocks in upstate New York for five years, and still I do not understand how most of them formed. And neither does anyone else.